RED & BLUE

A Memoir of Two Alaskan Tour Guides

Judy Shuler

Hildegard Ratliff

To Honey
my superior who encouraged
so much patience with
me and is always there for me — for all
of us.
Best wishes
Blue

Ouzel Press
Fredonia, New York

ISBN-978-0615622323

RED & BLUE

Also by Judy Shuler

Alaska Travel Planning Guide: Help for the
Independent Traveler

DEDICATION

To my husband Fred who supported my dream, to my fellow independent tour operators who helped insure our clients' trips exceeded their expectations, and to all visitors who allowed me to be a part of their travels in Alaska.

JS

I dedicate my portion of this book to my late husband Jerry, who had kept me rolling every day with a clean, maintained vehicle and to my children, grandchildren and great-grandchildren. A quote from my grandson Keith: "Every kid should experience Alaska just once." My heartfelt thanks to my friend Red, who coached me through all of it.

HR

CONTENTS

Page

STORIES FROM RED

STORIES FROM BLUE

ACKNOWLEDGMENTS

Thanks to Cheryl Probst, author of *DIY Beijing* and numerous other travel guides; Marge Hermans Osborn, author of numerous books about the natural history of Southeast Alaska; and to Kathleen Q. Weltzin, a voracious reader, for their editing and insightful suggestions.

Photos by Judy Shuler

INTRODUCTION

It was 1984. We didn't yet know each other. But we were both totally captivated by the place in which we lived. And we had each begun thinking about how we could forgo government jobs to share what we cherished with tourists. Eventually we met on the sidewalks of downtown Juneau, Alaska. Two people as different as red and blue forged a friendship as fast as it was unlikely.

With our separate businesses we offered photography tours, nature walks, tours to artists' studios. When cruise ships docked, arriving passengers glanced at our signs and walked right on by to their sightseeing bus. It would be another decade before nature tours and ecotourism caught on and people eagerly made it the fastest growing segment of the travel industry.

Gradually the future caught up with us. We found visitors who reveled in the same things we treasured about this place, and they found us.

This is our story, theirs and ours, and the story of the many who wander in response to a profound longing to connect with the natural world and with each other.

Alaska is and isn't the same place we inhabited with our visitors. It is no longer so mysterious as it was when we first started greeting tourists and they'd ask about the local currency or what kind of stamps to stick on postcards destined for other U.S. states. More recent events and personalities have brought it front and center on the world stage.

It is perhaps human nature that wherever we live, especially if we've been there a long time, we tend to think of it as unique. When we poke our nose into the wider world, we may discover it is not so singular after all.

Alaskans, and we plead guilty, seem particularly prone to that myopic view. But mountains, glaciers, icy roads, extreme weather, big animals, hunting and fishing are not exclusive to the 49th state.

What makes Alaska truly different, we think, is the sheer scale of it—the incomprehensible distances with all the ramifications of vast un-peopled areas, the mind-numbing vistas in every direction. While much of the American East has wild places surrounded by human development, Alaska has small enclaves of development surrounded by expansive wildness.

It is still that wildness, never far away and overshadowing all, that defines Alaska for residents and visitors alike.

1. Red and Blue Again—May 2002

I dressed deliberately, pulling a new red cotton knit tunic over black wool pants. It was my first purchase of anything red in the years since I'd left the sidewalks of downtown Juneau, Alaska—the first time I could bring myself to wear red again at all.

It felt good. I was detached now from that former life with all its intensity, its rewards and disappointments. I reached into a big covered glass jar in the bedroom closet I had converted to office shelves, pulled out an old pin, black and white, and pinned it on my chest. A local artist had designed my logo, a white raven with "Alaska Up Close" written in black over its rectangular back. "Juneau" arched across the top of the round pin in reverse type, "Alaska" curved around the bottom. It was an identity that once consumed my imagination, my energy, my life on the sidewalks and beyond. Eighteen years ago I had set out to claim my niche in the developing travel industry when the very name "Alaska" still seemed mysterious and exotic.

Now it was May 2002, and the first cruise ship of the season would soon arrive. The second of Juneau's three distinct seasons was about to begin. We all mark seasons by the pathway of the sun, the migration of birds, the succession of wildflowers and those we plant and tend. But this season is distinguished by the comings and goings of people. Lots of people. About 700,000 people who would stay for less than a day, in just over four months.

Our temperate rainforest itself doesn't change much, thanks to the Japanese ocean currents that bring warm winters, cool summers, and spring and fall that blend indistinguishably into both. There's typically a little snow in winter, a lot of rain every time else. Yet our seasons are more sharply delineated than, say, in North Dakota or Vermont.

The first season, January into April, is defined by our role as Alaska's capital city, when visitors are out-of-town legislators, staffers and the inevitable retinue of lobbyists who follow them. Soon after the legislature adjourns, cruise ships begin arriving, heralding the second season. The third season starts when the last ship sails south in late September, a respite from the intensity of the first two seasons when we reclaim the town as ours alone. I think of them as suits, ships and solitude.

This year the first ship was the *Norwegian Sky*, filled with pre-season bargain-seekers and travel agents cruising free in exchange for future bookings. Cruise ship cabins are more perishable than fresh raspberries. An empty cabin is revenue lost forever. Every cruise line is firmly fixed on filling every cabin on every sailing, even if it means giving some away to other members of the industry or discounting to a price less than the cost of staying home.

Perks from fellow members of the travel industry are eagerly sought, even expected. One summer a woman who said she was a travel agent approached me wearing a gold lamé raincoat, gold painted fingernails and gold jewelry. "Do you have anything free you can give me?" she asked. I wasn't in a league to give free tours to someone with questionable credentials, though I didn't put my refusal in quite those words. "Do you know anyone who could give me something?" she said plaintively as she walked away in search of someone else to ask.

The *Norwegian Sky* carried 2,020 passengers and 800 crew. It's a ratio designed to insure someone is always there to anticipate your every whim, to pamper you so outrageously that the ship becomes more important than your destination. And to our consternation—we who had sought to offer a more intimate look at the home we loved—their approach worked. Within five years of this day Juneau's summer cruise ship passenger count would near one million.

Dressed in remnants of our previous life, my former colleague and I drove nine miles from our homes in the Mendenhall Valley to the Juneau waterfront to meet the ship. It was a trip we had each driven countless times when our joint world revolved around this season. We had been independent tour operators back when it was still possible, before cruise ships became the Wal-Marts of the travel industry, sending small independent operators the way of mom and pop stores throughout the country.

This time I drove the white Grand Caravan SE I'd downsized to after 10 years; she rode shotgun. Today was just about memories, seeing old faces, reminding each other how glad we were to be out of the fray.

The downtown streets were nearly empty when Blue and I arrived for lunch. Scheduled docking was at least two hours away. We'd allowed time to walk past shopkeepers arranging shelves and hosing down sidewalks from a dusty spring.

Our first stop was a local jewelry shop, one of the oldest shops on South Franklin Street and one of the few downtown stores to remain open year around.

"We're enjoying watching all the other stores scurry around. We're ready," a clerk said with a touch of smugness.

Well, they were entitled. How many other tour businesses and shops had opened and closed while they had stayed the course?

They certainly outlasted me.

3

Two blocks away Blue and I slipped into a candle shop to admire shiny Christmas ornaments and candles of every hue.

"How do you like your new space?" I asked the owner. It was my subtle way of making sure we were not mistaken for tourists.

"We're going to be year-round just like always."

That was her way of distancing herself from summer-only shops that abandon downtown just minutes after the last ship sails in September. Local resentment of the summer-only shops is palpable.

Several stores spent the winter trading more space for more visibility. What had been the center of the downtown shopping district was now on the fringes. The cruise line that casts the longest shadow precipitated that when they built their own dock on private land beyond reach of the city center. Their every action sent ripples through every other player for blocks around and became a lightning rod for every aggravation that a huge industry can foist upon a town.

We headed for lunch in the bright blue Merchants Wharf, a seaplane hangar from the 1940s that now houses shops and restaurants on precarious-looking pilings. The largest restaurant is a favorite with locals for its picture windows overlooking the harbor, extravagantly portioned seafood platters and dozens of varieties of beer on tap. Once we shared a small office on the floor directly overhead.

The restaurant tables and booths were full, leaving us to a window counter that proved the best seat in the house.

Blue, who is tall with a large frame but still oozes sex appeal at an age you would not believe, wore a baseball cap over her short blond hair. Seeing her only from the back, the waitress schmoozed, "Hi, Guy." She hadn't noticed the crimson nails and a bosom to die for. It was an embarrassing mistake, but Blue took it in stride. She is not easily fazed. Today she was pensive. She had buried husband number six exactly a year ago.

"I miss him, but I like being free," she acknowledged. Freedom is not something you could feel with a guy like #6.

We ordered blackened halibut wraps and drank in the unfolding tableau beyond the enormous windows.

A huge pile of rock juts out into Gastineau Channel, the detritus of a long-closed gold mine known simply as the "Rock Dump." It was gold that converted a forest-covered mountainside to the backdrop for a town more than a hundred years ago. I watched over the top of the rocks for a tell-tale plume of smoke, a sure sign that a ship is approaching the harbor.

Our talk turned to the impending arrival, the way it did when it dictated our life on the dock. The diners around us were not so obsessed. "Is there a ship due today?" a 40-ish guy in a plaid shirt casually asked his lunch companion. Such is the divide over tourism in our town: investment and intense interest, versus indifference.

It was now an hour before the appointed arrival. A Coast Guard ship cruised the harbor, reflecting the new security, post 9/11.

How much was pro-active, we wondered?

"It's all show," Blue declared.

"What a tempting target," Blue said. Three-thousand people afloat in miles of undeveloped, un-peopled wildness. How hard could it be to crouch under a tree above, then lob an explosive downward? But people in positions to ponder such things seem to focus more on ports and harbors.

Once locals could simply stroll aboard ships in port, walk into a bar and order a drink. Then in 1985 American tourist Leon Klinghoffer was shot in his wheelchair by hijackers aboard the *Achille Lauro*. His name and that of the ship from which his body was cast into the Mediterranean Sea entered the international lexicon. Ships were suddenly off-limits to all but passengers and approved guests.

5

As we left the restaurant, the downtown streets that were void of traffic when we drove in for lunch were filling with buses, vans, cars and taxis. There was still time to check out a few shops, and we picked one that features mostly arts and crafts created in-state and offers clear views of the channel and approaching ships. Much Alaskan memorabilia is cloned out of state and on the other side of the Pacific, and we always promoted local shops and products when we could. The ship glided silently into view while I was head down over a glass display case, inspecting a sterling silver pin shaped like a loon. Blue spotted it, bolted out the door, and was across the street before I even looked up. She hadn't lost her old instinct. It kicked in seamlessly.

"Hey, Red, she's here," Blue said when I caught up with her on the dock.

"She" was a gleaming vision in white, with gulls flocking about the bow while eager passengers lined the railings four stories high. Blue waved at them and they waved back.

"Can you believe we used to do this every day?" she asked.

I couldn't. It seemed as remote as another lifetime.

"Take my picture in front of the ship," Blue said. Back when we were hustling the ships we would have already been at work, smiling, waving, making eye contact with passengers in the hope they would look for us on shore and buy our tour. There was no time for such frivolousness as taking our own pictures. Today I obliged, and we pressed a passerby to take a picture of us together.

People are naturally drawn to Blue, and they tend to tell her personal things. It is her gift. I talked to tourists about the height of the mountains and how a glacier moves; she told them about living in a cabin and how it feels to catch a fish—real life stuff.

Blue and I continued walking the wooden dock to mid-ship. We watched a small cluster of business people just ahead of us on the dock as they unfurled and held up a tired, wrinkled "Welcome to Juneau" oilcloth sign. Wearing perfunctory smiles, they were middle-aged guys who managed books and hired the staff members who actually interact with tourists.

We kept walking, past the Marine Parking Garage and Juneau Public Library where the shore side crowd was more electric. In a tiny compressed area like downtown Juneau, parking is at a premium. When a three-level parking garage was built along the waterfront it created plenty of discussion about the best use of waterfront property. Eventually a library with panoramic views was built on top of the garage, partly mollifying the opponents.

The structure is a central landmark downtown, bordering busy Marine Park and two of the five cruise ship docks. On the water side, routinely seen only by people from a ship or fishing boat, a mural painted by Dan DeRoux depicts passengers aboard the steamship *Ancon* arriving in Juneau in the late 1800s. He substituted faces of more recent residents with Juneau roots several generations deep like his. A steel sculpture by Juneau artist Ray Peck hung on the town side reflects indigenous Tlingit culture.

Veterans of our erstwhile industry greeted each other while fresh-faced youngsters strained at the starting gate of their first season. Were they mere kindergarteners when we started out?

We saw our first familiar face, the popular and outgoing former state director of tourism Don Dickey. He stopped to pose with Blue while I snapped their picture.

"He must be 80 by now," we guessed. A snowbird who wintered in Scottsdale, Arizona, he seemed as witty and full of stories as ever.

"When you get white on top like this, you need to go places while you still can," he said.

When he died at 89 in 2011 we remembered how he had tirelessly championed travel to Alaska and small operators like us as well as the industry giants who dominate today—and how together we had all been part of something fresh and exciting.

Nearby we saw Diane, a vivacious blond who had worked seven years for a flight-seeing operator and now greeted tourists as a volunteer. She bristles when locals complain about floatplane and helicopter noise, the most contentious of local tourism issues.

"I love the sounds of airplanes." She almost sang the words. "Sometimes I'll be talking on the phone and I'll have to say 'Just a minute,' but in 30 seconds it's over with."

Big tourism, like any big industry, has entered the daily life of the locals in a way it did not intrude when we began driving our vans to the dock and offering tours.

Diane had just wintered near a small town on the Oregon coast. She could walk the beach weekdays and see maybe five or six other people, she said. "On weekends you might see 20 people on the beach and you think 'Go away.' You didn't hear local people complaining about it, though."

"Twenty people," I thought. How about 2,000 people on one ship, times five? In one day? And not just on weekends? It didn't exactly seem the same. Now that I was no longer part of this scene I was wont to side with the locals. But it was time to move on.

Ahead was Donna, the co-owner of our old sightseeing competitor and nemesis. "There's what-do-you-call-'em? 'EMT?' " said Blue, who has changed careers from tourism to health care.

Well, she had two out of three letters right, but they were slightly out of order.

Blue and I had each driven our own vans; Donna was our arch competitor who oversaw a fleet of old school buses painted baby blue with white initials on the side. Today she looked the same as when she had first entered our world on the street, maybe a little heavier but otherwise the same: dark blond hair combed back and held by a sun visor, blue striped tank top, beige shorts. She was 44 now and had been selling tours on the sidewalks 15 years.

As our rival she taught us how to hustle, how to plan ahead and sell tours for a specific departure time rather than just pulling away from the dock when we thought we had as many passengers as we were likely to get. She forced us to cut our prices in half and eventually drove us off the street. Now we hugged and greeted each other like old friends.

Small scale operators like Blue and me are no longer part of the mix. Our municipal sales permits had cost us $100 per year. Now permits to sell tours dockside are meted out by competitive bid, effectively eliminating any low-volume operator with the kind of individualized tours we offered. Our competitor told us she bid $11,000 this year, more than we would have netted in an entire season.

While we could prop a sign against a mountain ash tree or set up a portable sign on the sidewalk in the little park where passengers came ashore, vendors were now caged in tiny kiosks next to the parking garage.

"They look like two-hole outhouses without the door," I told Blue. We watched freshly minted, automated smiles and heard a chipper "Welcome to Juneau."

We once did that, I thought incredulously.

When I first picked up the hand-held microphone that carried my voice to the back of the 14-passenger van, I was determined it would be a natural conversation, just me describing my hometown to visiting friends. I would talk about the misty days I loved, the mild winters that no one expected here, the black bear that once scaled our backyard five-foot chain-link fence, leaving behind a tooth-marked salmon and an enormous pile of scat.

Had I mentioned the tides that could change 20 vertical feet every six and one-half hours? Within weeks of doing a daily monologue, I couldn't remember. Did I tell them about the bald eagles I looked for every day? That a day without an eagle was like a day without sunshine? I didn't recall. Clearly I would need cues. At Lemon Creek, where low tide could drain a saltwater channel into a grassy meadow, I would talk about tides. Where the highway yielded glimpses of northern Admiralty Island, I would talk about brown bear living in population densities of one per square mile. In short, I would have a script.

The black and white pin I wore today was left over from pins we gave to our passengers at the beginning of the tour. Many offered to give them back when it was over. We said they were for promotion, and I urged them to wear the pins in perpetuity or take them home to grandchildren. In reality we used them so we could recognize people when they returned to our van after a 30-minute stop at the Mendenhall Glacier visitor center, then smile as though we remembered their faces.

I never thought it would be that way. Who couldn't remember for 30 minutes what six or eight or 10 people looked like? I remembered engaging conversations, voices, stories of where they came from—why not faces? Except for a few who remain vivid to this day, they blended together, for the most part indistinguishable.

It all felt as distant today as though it never happened at all. Maybe I'd read about in it a magazine. Surely it wasn't me.

I only remember the day I finally realized the industry had changed and my life on the sidewalks of downtown Juneau was over. It was all I knew, all I worked for, dreamed about, for years. What now? What would I do with the rest of my life?

Blue and I stopped for dessert and coffee after the ship was secured at the dock and our old colleagues had to tend to business just as we once did. Blue wanted ice cream, but the restaurants were out. We settled for coffee and split a piece of chocolate decadence pie at a Mexican restaurant, and watched with detachment as tourists begin streaming by the window on their way to shop.

"I'm sick of tourists already," Blue said.

2. Back to 1984

As decades go, the 1980s have a lot to answer for. The Me Decade. Greed. Big hair. Yuppies. *Dynasty* and *Dallas*. Power suits. What were we thinking?

Here we were not immune, but we were not totally caught up in it all either. There was, and remains, a lingering sense that in mindset as well as geography, Alaska stands somewhat apart. That every place else is "Outside"—our self-absorbed term for any place other than Alaska—and the things that matter there may not matter here.

Back in 1984 I spent $4,000 for an apple-red and white Ford Econoline 350 van. It had a cracked windshield and catsup smeared inside the driver side beige door panel. The catsup was easy, the windshield set me back $372.48. I had driven past a waterfront inn where it was parked all winter, looking at the "For Sale" sign on the driver's side window and imagining it was mine. The van would be my entrée into the realm of tourism. It would be my escape from a government office job I didn't want in an awkward box of a building I didn't like.

It was time to set my ideas in motion.

On my last day at work, April 15, I invited co-workers to a four-mile ride in my van, its maiden voyage with me at the wheel. I provided the fixings for an early spring picnic: soda, chips, bread, cold cuts and condiments, at a scenic pull-off called Suicide Falls. It would be the first of many stops there in the years ahead. The raven logo with my business name, Alaska Up Close, was already painted on each side and the back doors, and a small hand-held microphone and front and back speakers from a local audio store ($406.76) were in place. Though mostly taken aback by the venture I'd kept secret until submitting a written resignation just two weeks earlier, everyone seemed to wish me well. One co-worker offered sage advice for maneuvering a 14-passenger van: steer the front end and the rear will follow. Could it be that simple? Yes it was, but I remembered it well in some tight navigation to come.

There was no registry, no formal training. With a business license, insurance, and permits from the City and Borough of Juneau and U.S. Forest Service in hand, I was a tour guide. It was the latest incarnation in my long, spectacularly non-lucrative, quest for self-employment: dressmaker, free-lance writer, portrait photographer, and now this.

When my business was no more than an idea, I had queried owners and employees of other local tourism businesses for ideas and insights. A couple who'd met cruise ships the year before I started said their business records were all in their check book. "Look at someone's check book," a Methodist minister said in one of the few sermons I've remembered over the years, "and I'll tell you what's important to them." Right now, my check book was all about this idea I was bringing to life.

A bank account with my business name and the ledger book I'd set up after completing local university classes in marketing and administration for small business told the story of my plans: State business license, $25; the local city and borough's certificate of convenience and necessity (a name that always struck me as odd) $125. Record-keeping for a small business, $70; marketing class for small business, $45. There was another

$300 for membership in a regional tourism association and a small ad in their visitor guide. U.S. Forest Service outfitter-guide permit for driving people to the Mendenhall Glacier parking lot, $275. Physician's exam for local chauffeur's license, $33. So far the expense side of the ledger totaled $5,652.24.

Back in 1984 ecotourism didn't yet have a name, and nature tours were geared to hard-core birders and wilderness explorers. Photo tours and workshops with celebrity outdoor photographers were still in the future. First Friday art gallery openings hadn't yet spread across the country. Alaska tourism was a whisper of what it would become.

In Juneau I was planning art shows, monthly programs and field trips for our local chapter of the National Audubon Society. Surely tourists would enjoy these same things, I thought. And they could get a glimpse of the real Alaska they had come to see.

My tour business would specialize in nature walks, nature photography and artist tours, I decided. We would walk the trails I'd discovered through the Juneau Audubon Society, identifying birds, wildflowers and berries and watching for wildlife. In my small way I'd lend economic value to wildlife and wetlands in their natural state. I would take visitors to the studios of local artists whose work I admired. They would share cookies and coffee with Alaskans who shined a light on the north through their art.

---

1. It's Okay

I got my mandatory physical exam from a retired local physician for $25. Then in his late 80s, he held a bottle of urine specimen against the light of a window in his hilltop home in downtown Juneau. "It's okay," he said. He was a downhill skier at Eagle Crest Ski Area even in his 90s.

I designed blank forms to carry on a clip board next to my seat. "Daily Trip Report," it read across the top. Along with lines to fill in odometer readings, departure and return times and locations, and number of passengers, I added space for weather, sightings of birds, animals and wildflowers, comments from passengers. A ball point pen on a cotton cord around my neck insured a pen was always at hand.

A red plastic egg crate fit exactly between the driver and front passenger seats. It was just right to hold binoculars, nature guidebooks and rolled nautical maps.

I imagined my passengers thumbing through my on-board library. *The National Audubon Society Field Guide to North American Wildflowers: Western Region. Seashells of North America. Wild Edible and Poisonous Plants of Alaska. Wildflowers of Alaska* by Christine Heller. Bob Armstrong's *Guide to the Birds of Alaska. Animal Tracks of Alaska.* We'd go to my favorite places for photographing flowers and landscapes. I knew when and where to find shooting stars, sea stars or salmonberries because for several years I'd been making notes in a desk calendar for my own pleasure. I'd had no idea how useful they would one day be to a tour guide.

I'd take my passengers to the best vantage points to photograph our main attraction, the Mendenhall Glacier. In the back of my van, under the back bench, I would slide my camera tripod and a Bausch and Lomb 20-60 mm zoom spotting scope in a long black case for close up bird viewing. A black vinyl backpack held my Nikon F2 35 mm camera, with 28 mm, 55 mm and 210 mm lens. In pre-digital days this was, except for wildlife photography, a dream system.

I had thought long and hard about a name that would express my perspective and what I wanted to offer: an intimate look at this place that made me count just living here as the gift of a lifetime. I wanted it to be genuine, not plasticized blather for tourists. I wanted to give insights that only a full-time resident could offer. "Up close," I decided. It needed to be broad enough to expand to services beyond my home town to the entire state. Alaska. Alaska Up Close. In an alphabetical listing it would come near the top. I was pleased with the choice, and in no mood to have it taken over by someone who liked it as much as I did. I registered my business name for five years (cost, $25). While some operators tried to fly beneath the radar, I wanted to do everything right, by the rules. I wanted to

2. It Starts With an Idea

Everything starts with an idea and also with an opportunity. At the time we started I was working for the State of Alaska. Some people were laid off, and more work was added to our position. Then we saw the tour ships coming in and we thought it would be nice doing something outside with the tourists. That's actually how we started in the business.

And now the next thing that comes up is—well, we need something that these people can ride in. I mean, I needed some kind of a vehicle. I'd never driven a van before and my husband was very helpful. He knew his friend had a logging truck down in the state of Washington. That friend was more than willing to send that logging Suburban up here. Well, it arrived and when I opened up the back it was filled with mud. You know, people in the logging business, people hauling anything and everything and themselves; it was for the crew, actually. There was a lot of mud in there, the brakes didn't work, so we had to really do some scrubbing and polishing on that thing.

Now what are we going to do? We need brochures, licenses. At that time the business license was $25. Oh gosh, you need insurance too, you need liability and all that stuff. Got all that and did a couple of trial runs. Studied little bit about Juneau, the history, and also I

be able to grow and expand, even though I didn't know how at the time.

But the record-keeping was the mundane part. I directed most of my energy toward what I could do to set my tours apart, to give people a reason to choose me and then to make them glad they did.

I thought a lot about what I would tell people about this place that so captivated my own imagination. I studied nature

---

needed to know more about the plants, about the vegetation, because everything looked different from everywhere else I had lived.

There were different shrubberies and all these different trees and bushes, different ferns and stuff up here. So I took a college class, a three credit course in biology. That was in the fall, and it worked out okay. I did my lab work and all that was fine. But come summer I'm looking at these plants and I didn't know one from the other. They were all dead in the fall and they looked different now. But you keep learning.

I took a tour with another company and it sounded like they had a canned tour or something. Well, I think they all learned it down in the state of Washington and came up here and tried to identify these posies and everything else that was around here. That's how it was.

So then we talked to some of the local people and ventured out more. I mean, I started from scratch. My husband was very helpful at the time. He kept the vehicle clean and things like that.

Now it came to printing brochures and pricing it. That part was fun. Now advertisement, that was a little toughie. So what I did, I stood with an umbrella in Marine View Park and we watched for these ships to come in—you know, tried to be first one on the dock, and had a little black board, or in my case a white board, and we wrote down "Glacier Tours for $20."

So that's how we started.

But that got kind of boring, just glacier runs. After that I went to Germany and I thought, well, I'm going to promote some German tours, which I did. I already named my business German Connection Fototour. And I managed to get some groups in here and I couldn't take all the groups in one van, I mean I didn't even have a van yet. I just had that Suburban. I think I got the van two years later. And so my friend, I called her Red, I asked her if she would help with the German groups because I can't take them all. And she said "Well, I can't speak German." I said "That's okay. We'll make several stops, I'll get out and do my thing, and tell them what's what and it will work that way." And it did.

And we really did work together. And when she had a larger group is when I helped her also. And everyone thought we were rivals but we weren't.

We talked about marketing and everything else. Later on we had an office and that's when I asked my granddaughter Tanya to come up. She spent the summer with us, (the season is about three months) and she helped answering calls in the office. This was

---

guidebooks, read books about natural history and historical biographies, absorbed local events from the newspaper.

Then I drove the route I would take in my private car, practicing what I would say. To rehearse in front of an audience I joined a local Toastmasters club. I took my turn at being Toastmaster for the day, even served as president. For a speech in my manual I picked up an automobile rear view mirror, sat on the end of a table with my back to the audience

all before cell phones and computers. She wrote out letters; they were mailed, and it was by snail mail in comparison to what we have today. She helped book the tours also, helped passengers get on board, helped promote and she was great. This happened for a couple of years.

We had CBs but they didn't work around the mountains. Tanya says "Remember, Grandma, I was beeping you and you did not get my signal." Well, I was at Eaglecrest Ski Area with a group on top of the mountain. Tanya was trying to entertain people, a family, hoping I would return soon. I didn't make it in time. Disappointed, they left.

"I wrote letters to clients, folded a brochure in it and mailed stuff out," she remembers. "I had an electric typewriter, answered phones for Red and Blue, took messages, booked clients and helped guide clients to their van. I remember one summer I got to lay out in the sun one time and the temperature was 65 degrees."

Now Tanya is working with a corporation in Denver, and scheduling all travel is among her duties. I keep telling her, "Remember where you got your start. . . ."

And then we had another granddaughter come up, my husband's granddaughter, Shannon. She did the same work and did a great job.

---

and looked at my fellow Toastmasters in the mirror while I a tried out my spiel. I imagined myself driving along Egan Expressway, the main highway linking downtown with the outlying community. I visualized what I and my passengers would see through the windshield as I drove, and took my audience for a virtual ride as I talked about the nature of this place. It was, in just one speech, the culmination of why I'd joined Toastmasters.

In the process I'd witnessed the power of the Toastmasters' program to change lives, including my own. One tall good-looking young man came into a meeting with a shyness that has crippled many an aspiration. The confidence he found over time would empower him to head his neighborhood association and rise to the top of a state government agency. I learned I could go from quiet with few words to a 90-minute non-stop monologue, chipper, sometimes even funny. As one tour bus driver used to say as he swung into the driver's seat, "It's show time." I was ready for the spotlight.

It's something of a wonder I ended up here, 4,000 miles from where I grew up, given my general aversion to travel. I like being somewhere new, but not so much the process of getting there. Perhaps we all come with a blueprint that has little or nothing to do with upbringing. How else could children in the same family be so different? If that is so, my blueprint came with a compass pointing N. Tropical beaches and warm deserts that call to millions held no sway with me. Northern climates and landscapes and people seemed more vital. I liked their energy, the way you have to work a little harder just in the course of daily living, even in town and especially in remote places. The movie that called me was not South Pacific, but Doctor Zhivago. Once I traveled north, a few years out of school, I knew I was home.

Now, nearly two decades later, with my tour business, I would meet people from around the world who also felt the tug northward, though they would often tell me they could never imagine living here. They would expand my world in ways I had not yet imagined, and I wouldn't have to pack.

Tuesday, May 15, 1984, was sunny with a low of 40 degrees F. and a high in the mid 60s. It was a stellar day in our coastal rainforest where, on nearly any given day, odds are better than 50 percent it will rain. The Cunard Princess, first cruise ship of the season, would dock at 2 p.m. The captain and crew would be met by the high school pep band and the U.S. Coast Guard color guard, by our mayor, who sang soprano in the same church choir where I sang alto, and by a gold rush dance revue in satin dresses with lace petticoats and feather boas. Despite its impressive welcome, the imminent arrival of the 1984 season had rated six paragraphs in the local newspaper the previous day, half of them on page 16. It was perfunctory coverage for a story that didn't affect a lot of people. State of Alaska employees made up most of the work force. Cruise ship tourism had not yet run into the buzz saw of local sentiment that lay ahead.

I drove downtown early, stretched and breathed deep on the sidewalk along the waterfront, looked around at the buses and people who shared these streets and thought "Okay, this is my new office. This is where I will come to work every day for the next four months."

Counterparts gradually showed up, too, most as green as I was. The young driver of a black limousine, dressed in a top hat and tailcoat. The round-faced son of a tourism marketing specialist we called The Kid, who drove a blue and white van in the same model as my red and white one. A quirky taxi and tour driver in what would become her uniform, gray sweat pants, plaid flannel shirt, and a red umbrella with a yellow duck bill and big black and white eyes. There was the Aviator, a taxi driver in a brown leather jacket. And there was Blue.

Blue and I were the most unlikely of collaborators. Blue seemed to me as exotic as any of the people we met from aboard the ships, or even the ships themselves. She had a past I could not even imagine. I had a quiet conservative upbringing in the bucolic Midwest. Blue came of age in Germany in the midst of war. I married once; she negotiated a checkerboard of tragic romances that encircled the globe. She was warm when life could have easily rendered her cold. One who draws people in and makes them feel safe.

21

Against my measured, studied, calculated approach, she brought street-smarts and taught me more than I could ever have imagined.

We had cryptic names for ourselves and just about everyone else in our world. Most people and things can be summarized in one or two words of four letters or less if you squeeze out everything superfluous. Your own life experience fills in around the edges. Think of the power words: love, hate, fear, joy, war, art. Anyone can bring out the obscure multi-syllable words and try to sound like they know more than they do. But to really find the essence, that is genius.

She was Blue, I was Red.

"You have to have a gimmick," we kept saying. For me, with a closet full of gray and black, it evolved into wearing all red to match my red and white 14-passenger van—or at least red as far as the eye could see. Red rubber boots for the frequent rainy days, red felt hat, red cable knit Eddie Bauer wool sweater, red chino pants, red nylon quilted vest, red duster raincoat, all to stand out on the docks as I hawked my tours. For rare warm sunny days I had red culottes, a short-sleeved knit top and red running shoes. For every day I had plastic red hoop earrings, six-sided, not too big, not too small. Shopping trips inevitably included the eternal search for red. Blue, with her blue van, was as blue as I was red.

My first uniform wasn't red at all. I'd made two jump suits, one gray, one gold, to wear over turtlenecks, my wardrobe staple in Alaska since my arrival two decades earlier. I had long ago settled on Lands' End turtles, not only for their sturdy

---

3. My First Passengers

I remember only one thing about my first passengers. They paid in Canadian dollars.

resolve in the face of weekly laundering, but partly, I think, because their name seemed so right for this place. But after a few weeks of drinking copious cups of coffee while waiting for ships to arrive and dock, then peeling off layers of rain jacket, sweatshirt and jumpsuit to pass it off, I knew it was time for a more functional approach.

I wish I could recall my very first passengers—where they lived, what it felt like to pull away from the curb for the first time, whether I was nervous. Surely I was. My first trip reports were discarded in a fit of housecleaning years ago.

Sometimes I'd set up the spotting scope I'd bought to focus on eagles next to my sign advertising my tours, but it wasn't the big draw I'd hoped it would be. More successful—brilliant even, and totally unfair, I thought—was the ploy of a competitor who brought her dog to the dock. Next to bringing out a baby to remind travelers of grandchildren left at home, the dog was guaranteed to elicit an "Aw, gee," and sales.

Our biggest competitors were not each other, but the cruise ships who carried them to our docks. Most passengers booked their local tours aboard ship, when their cruise began.

"They told us on board that if we didn't book their tours we couldn't see anything. Now we wish we'd waited," many told us during our years on the dock. One passenger told us he inquired on board about getting a taxi upon arrival in Juneau, and was told Juneau didn't have any taxis. It would take 22 years for Alaskan voters to pass a law requiring cruise ships to reveal they receive a commission for the tours they sell on board, and that alternatives might be available on shore. Those who hadn't bought the ship's tours, typically people who had cruised before, would look us over, ask each of us where our tour went and what it cost, then select one of us and gamely climb into our vehicle for a local tour.

We spent much of that first summer looking through the windows of each other's vehicles, to see who was getting most of the leftovers. Somehow we all got a share. Cut-rate bus tours to compete with cruise ship shore excursions (and us) were still a year away. We were all friends.

All except the Aviator.

He was tall, stocky, with thick curly red hair and a full baby face peppered with freckles. Blue and I conferred his nickname because of his ever-present brown leather aviator jacket with lamb's wool collar, worn open over tight blue jeans.

Lord, how vivid he still remains in my mind!

Cool, confident, smirky, he was the first cab driver in Juneau to realize he could make more money hauling tourists than hauling drunks by proclaiming himself a tour guide. Tourists smelled better and gave bigger tips.

The vibes between us were immediate. If I hadn't thought much about past lives and karma before, it wouldn't take much to convince me now. He lied, lied, lied, but all of his lies were directed toward me.

Our vehicles were usually parked next to each other along the curb reserved for independent tour vendors—his taxi, my van.

When I told potential passengers I would take them to all the usual must-see tourist spots, the Aviator would come behind me and tell them I just did birds. Or he'd say I charged more than I actually did. I was too upset to confront him.

One day a pine siskin—a non-descript little brown streaked finch—was impaled on the front grill of my van. The Aviator laughed and laughed.

"That woman does birding tours with a dead bird on her grill," he pointed out gleefully to passersby before I knew it was there. I must have hit it on the drive into town, I thought.

I seethed, and my resentment knew no bounds. "Do you think he planted it there?" Blue asked me years later. Even in my exasperation I hadn't considered that.

I ignored the Aviator. I refused to say good morning or even acknowledge his presence. I'd never felt that kind of anger before, and I had no idea how to deal with it.

I had never done anything remotely like this tour business before, and I don't mind saying I was scared. Determined, but scared. I'd just invested money, my imagination and heart and soul. A spare bedroom was fully converted to a home office, and I had to make this work.

Gradually I came to realize it was not so much about confronting him as about confronting myself. Relationships can be like that, even the most intimate ones. Less about them and more about you. But it would take me longer than one summer to come to that understanding.

Meanwhile, several events of 1984 would shape that season and reach into today.

A proposal to capture orcas generated more public response than any other issue to date. A piece of public art was sent into exile. Fire struck a landmark downtown hotel. A raging river of mud hurtled 1,800 feet down a mountainside. A haunting poem was set to music. We heard early warnings of climate change. At the time, they felt like just more news of the day.

3. Downtown—Who and Where We Are

Southeast Alaska is the long arm that dangles limply off mainland Alaska in the lower right corner of the map, abutting Canada's northern British Columbia.

Other regions of Alaska barely recognize Southeast as a part of the state. The self-image Alaskans nurture is more tied to Mt. McKinley than to Glacier Bay, more to the crisp hard edge of cold than to the misty, mild, squishy rainforest. I understand that because when I lived in Anchorage I was part of that mindset. Southeast was something you flew over on the way "Outside," our self-absorbed term for any place other than Alaska. It surely wasn't a place you'd want to set down.

I expected to live and die in Anchorage. I once read that people are about 30 when they begin to grasp the idea that they are mortal and will one day die. On flights home to visit family and friends I used to be terrified that I might die away from my beloved home of heart. And when I was uprooted, as it felt, by my husband's work as an auditor, I was not immediately smitten by my new home of Juneau. Only over time did I succumb to the charms of a town at least a generation older than the one I'd left behind and to its gauzy, sensual landscape. Although both are coastal ports, Anchorage didn't feel that way. It sets its gaze inward to the land mass that is the source of its weather and its identity. I embraced Juneau as a coastal town that felt and smelled like one, with all the possibilities that water brings.

Our Southeast towns all hug the shorelines. They flow sinuously around the bases of mountains, spill with abandon into valleys and tentatively climb vertical slopes. In downtown Juneau, mountain and beach are sometimes less than a block apart.

These are not the drive-to mountains of Denver, but in-your-face mountains that grab big chunks of sky, hovering so close one winter resident felt they might lean forward and absorb her into their dark foreboding depths. Dense evergreen forest climbs 3,000 feet skyward from sea level, until winter weather has its say. Above tree-line, summer alpine slopes are covered with ground-hugging blueberries, salmonberries, false hellebore, dwarf dogwood and bluebells. In winter they're buried by a hundred feet of snow and battered by winds that would qualify as Level 4 hurricanes on the Atlantic coast.

We have beaches where the mountains concede, but you can forego a bikini wax and leave Sunblock 40 at home. Rocks, rain pants, sweatshirts and rubber boots hold sway. The only sandy beach is detritus from gold mining, the ground-up tailings discarded after gold was extracted by adding mercury or cyanide more than a century ago.

A labyrinth of waterways and steep forested islands separates the Juneau waterfront from the open Pacific Ocean about 80 miles west. The Gastineau Channel that divides downtown Juneau on the mainland of North America from nearby Douglas Island is a narrow ribbon of ocean. A clean arch bridge spans the channel in about four-tenths of a mile, just 700 yards. You can walk it in minutes, even allowing time for paying homage to a pair of bald eagles who perch on power poles mid-channel—and for sweeping glances of downtown homes, shops and office buildings and of barges, kayaks, fishing boats and cruise ships plying channel waters.

Yet our bridge is more than twice as long as the 309-yard London Bridge over the River Thames. I was greatly surprised when I first saw the Thames, where events along seemingly every foot of river bank have inspired history books, novels, theater and cinema. Lady Jane Gray beheaded at the Tower of London in 1553 after nine days as queen. The Globe Theatre burning in 1613 from cannon fire during a performance of *Henry VIII*. St. Paul's Cathedral dating back to A.D 604. How could a place with so much history seem so . . . small?

But then, does London have more history? While Romans were invading and plundering, indulging their hedonistic side at Bath, Tlingit Indians along this channel were trading furs and tools, raiding other tribes for slaves, telling stories, writing songs and choreographing dances. On two sides of the world, one bordering the Atlantic Ocean, the other the Pacific, people were making love, having babies, dying brave and foolish deaths, loving and hating their family and neighbors.

It is along water that so much human history plays out, where life is writ large. The River Liffey, dividing Dublin between the haves and the have-nots. Niagara Falls, still attracting honeymooners, though the wild free-flowing falls were cut to half their original volume to harness hydropower for New York City. The Inland Sea, five great lakes that encapsulate the world's largest fresh surface water system as it touches two nations, two provinces and eight states.

Water in all its forms seeks us out and draws us in, alternately soothing, awing and terrifying us. But it is in standing where land meets sea that our spirit is enlarged and we see a world without limits.

There were two main docks in Juneau where passengers moved from sea to shore. The primary one was in Marine Park, a small downtown waterfront park with trees encircled by concrete, benches and a grassy knoll. As ships eased into the downtown dock, we staked out our sites. Mine was a mountain ash tree in clear view of the upcoming stream of disembarking passengers. Leaning against the trunk I readied a white eraser board sign, printing with red and blue markers the details of my tour: "City & Glacier, 2 ½ hours, $20."

Those who hadn't booked a tour on board, and were traveled enough to know they'd likely find alternatives on shore, would stop and inquire about our offerings. One man dutifully interviewed every one of us who operated a van or taxi tour, then led his wife away by the hand and said they'd "pray about it." I'm not sure if he climbed into another vehicle that day; I only remember I was not the answer to his prayers.

"Where are you from?" I'd begin by asking that after I'd loaded my van as full as I imagined it would get. People were usually eager to say, and to learn what common bond they might have with fellow passengers in the van.

They came from California, Arizona, Florida, places with hot dry summers. Some came from New Zealand, Great Britain, Mexico, and sprinkled across the continental United States.

"We'll start downtown," I'd tell them as we pulled away from the curb and turned onto South Franklin Street, core of the gift shop area. It was also the heart of the town that gold built, with buildings still surviving from the early 1900s. Juneau came into being in this unlikely place, I'd explain, because gold was found here in 1880. I told them how lucky we were that while early wood frame buildings of other small towns had been lost to fire, ours had escaped such ravage.

"Gold miners worked in three shifts around the clock, and this street was always alive with off-duty miners. The mines closed two days a year, on Christmas and the Fourth of July. When the pounding of the stamp mill stopped the quiet was deafening."

29

The Juneau gold belt arcs along the coastline for some 100 miles, and I assured them it hadn't all been mined yet. Sometimes that sparked more than just a passing interest. Nuggets found in nearby Gold Creek a century ago testified to the presence of gold, but if you're after the mother lode you have to grind up a lot of rock. For the Alaska Juneau Gold Mining Company, operating on the mountainside just south of downtown, that translated into crushing 13,000 tons of ore per day and nearly 90 million tons of rock and ore over its operation from 1893 to 1944. As we drove through downtown I'd show them what happened to all that left-over rock.

"They did hard rock mining," I'd explain. "The ground up rock was combined with mercury, which bonded to the gold. Then they'd chemically separate the gold from the mercury and dump the tailings along the waterfront." At some point I'd make sure we got a good view of the side of Mt. Roberts, with its skeletal steel and concrete remains of the mining operation. I'd tell them about the downtown Emporium building, where they could see mural-size photos of the mine buildings as they looked before the mines closed in 1944 and before the last remnants were lost in fire in the 1960s. I explained the ore came from the Last Chance and Silverbow Basins between Mt. Juneau and Mt. Roberts just behind town, and it was carried to tidewater for processing via layers of rail tracks inside Mt. Roberts.

And I'd tell them there were more miles of rail tunnels inside that mountain than miles of roadway within the entire city outside.

"This was once the red light district," I'd say as we passed false-front buildings now selling more tangible products. They smiled and no doubt imagined a far distant past. But a local artist remembers delivering the newspaper to brothels as a child in the 1950s, and feeling quite safe under the protective eyes of their residents.

30

The first two blocks inland from the waterfront are now given over mostly to summer visitors, with a few year-round jewelers, a movie theater, bars, restaurants, coffee shops and dress shops in the mix. Passengers in Blue's van might have heard her tell about when she bartended at the Triangle Club, on the corner of Front and South Franklin Streets.

One dress shop, now closed, found its daily bread in evening gowns for cruise ship passengers who may have come without formal wear for captain's night dinner, or who simply wanted a gown from afar for next season's holiday parties. Another, still thriving, features younger, trendier clothes than you're apt to see on the average local, who favors the more functional Gortex hooded jacket and sweatshirts. Once there were men's clothing stores, a hardware store, a department store and an office supply store; as in other cities such retailers have retreated from the heart of town to the fringes.

Back in 1984, South Franklin Street was a bit seedy, run-down at the heels and a genuine source of amazement to tourists when told they were in the state capital. It looked as if it needed a good bath and a haircut and some new clothes, something you could photograph for the front of a color brochure. When ships started arriving in numbers to support new tourist businesses, government and industry saw the future and shook hands. The spruce-up began.

What followed were new sidewalks, nylon banners with whimsical depictions of Juneau history, flora and fauna, and baskets of bright flowers hung from old-fashioned metal light poles painted deep turquoise. Sidewalks morphed to pedestrian-friendly widths. It was the beginning of the "new" historic district, with newly constructed and remodeled false-front buildings in shades of limes and cantaloupe, lemons and lilacs joining the authentically old ones. South Franklin Street shops now proffer tee-shirts, postcards, trinkets from China, the same jewelry you'll find in ports of call in the Caribbean, and on occasion a piece of Alaskan art or jewelry you'd include in your will.

It's called the old part of town but it reflects a highly romanticized view of what was. Did gutsy gold miners who spent 12-hour shifts in dangerous mine shafts deep inside mountains over a century ago really spend their free time in buildings the color of orange or pineapple sherbet? It doesn't seem likely. Locals sneer "Disneyland," but tourists seem to like them. Mickey had set foot in the north and we invited him to stay. And who is to say that's totally a bad thing? Reality can be highly over-rated. But I'm still glad I led tours when downtown was grittier and more real.

I'd point out Juneau's most famous saloon, the Red Dog, as we drove by. When we were hustling tours on the sidewalk, there were two questions we could count on: "Where are the restrooms?" and "Which way is the Red Dog?"

"Why is it world famous?" someone would invariably ask. "They have a good press agent," I'd say lightly. Actually, their press agents were legion. They were the many ships' crew members who were warmly welcomed inside and then reciprocated by spreading the word to passengers throughout the season, year after year.

A likely predecessor—the lineage is uncertain—was called Bucket O' Blood, which you can feel fairly certain had a storied history. Back in 1984, the Red Dog was a real bar, where fishermen lifted one next to bureaucrats, and tourists were allowed brief entry into their world. The space was rented, the floor was crooked, there were issues with sprinklers and safety and handicap accessibility. Before long it moved to its own brand-new building a block and one-half away, carrying its sawdust and artifacts and myths with it .

Tourists still want to sit in the saloon, have their pictures taken outside its swinging doors and go inside for a pricey beer or "duck fart." The latter, a big seller, appeals to the same frontier sensibility as swizzle sticks and dangle earrings made of shellacked moose droppings. The drink was reportedly invented by a bartender in Anchorage, but the claim is questionable given the variations of recipes now on the internet from around the world. A duck fart is easy to make: take a shot glass and layer, in order, Kalùha, Bailey's Irish Cream and Crown Royal.

But like so many things, the setting is all, and serving one up at home is far from the same. The saloon's biggest seller is a story for later.

"This is all on fill," I'd say of the street as I drove slowly past shops while impatient cars trailed behind. "Mine tailings were dumped along the waterfront to make the town site bigger." My little business was too small to warrant commissions, so I'd just point out the shops I liked myself. A feathered eagle Christmas tree ornament, made of chicken feathers in China, hung from my rear view mirror. It always attracted attention.

"There's the shop where you can buy one," I told passengers as we drove past a store specializing in Christmas ornaments. With limited time in port, passengers would sometimes buy mine and I'd have to replace it. I should have marked up the price, I reason now. I was better at thinking up new ideas for my tour than making money.

"There on the right you can buy classy sweatshirts and tee shirts that you'll still wear after you're back home," I'd say as we traveled up the street. Things that seem terribly funny on any vacation have a way of ending up in a wad at the back of a drawer. There's clearly a market, but how often would you wear a tee-shirt with a drawing of the rear end of a sled dog team and the slogan "Who farted?"

"On your left is a gift shop with really neat things, not the usual trinkets," I continued, smudging the side window as I jabbed my finger against the glass. Later, word circulated on the

4. Coney Islands

I wasn't even looking for this job at the Triangle Club. I was sitting with my girlfriend at the bar and they happened to have the polka music on and we started singing in German and just had a good time. It happened during the lunch hour and there were many people from the state building—that place was always packed from the people working for the state. They were having a beer, they were having you name it. They were eating, they were having this hot dog.

I remember my very first order after I was hired. He asked for a Coney Island.

I said "A Coney Island, what's in that?" I thought he meant some kind of drink.

You could have chili on it. On my days off I cooked sauerkraut and we put that on it too. It was a sauerkraut dog. Papa told me once they had originated on Coney Island. Electrocuted hot dogs, we called 'em. They have those hot dogs still today and they're still rotating in the window.

I worked for the Triangle from 1976 to 1978. In the 1970s female bartenders first started working at the Triangle and I was one of the first female bartenders.

Papa Joe was the owner of the bar. He was well-respected in the community. Papa came to the Territory, it was not then yet a state, in 1938. He acquired the Triangle Club in 1947. Papa taught me a lot about the miners, the loggers, and the fishermen. He had stored in his safe at the Triangle many beautiful gold nuggets and so had every other bar owner in Juneau. But Papa had most of them and the stories that went with them. He'd been prospecting before he came to Juneau. After Papa's death his son took over and I worked for him for two more years. And I also met my husband at the Triangle. There was also a barbershop adjacent to the bar. It was just like a rotating business.

Many came in and played pinochle. In the afternoon, about 4 to 5 o'clock was when we really did get busy with the workers. The construction workers came in, the loggers came in, the fishermen came in when they were in town. It was a working man's place, a working man's bar.

At that time you could leave your billfold on the bar; sometimes they would leave the money on the bar, go somewhere else, go across the street and have a drink and they knew when they came back everything was there. No one would even think about taking or stealing money or anything. They'd come in and say buy So-and-So a drink, or 6-pack the bar. Booze and money were just flowing at that time. We did have some people coming down for R&R. Ferry workers came in, I believe they were working one week on, one week off. In the evening we had a couple of male bartenders. When one of them left, and later on started working for my husband, I started working the night shift.

Cruise ships were coming in and they found out there was a German lady bartending at the Triangle so they came in and we had a great business with the *Prinsendam* at the time. I had the crew and the purser in from the *Prinsendam* and they did everything Dutch German Style. The custom here is that you pay for every drink that you order but not so in Europe. You just get a tab at the end of the evening and you just pay one time, pay everything together. In Germany they would make scratches on the coaster every time they deliver you a beer or whatever. They wanted the same thing done here, the crew. They said "Can you run a tab?" I thought "Oh, my God."

They ran a tab and kept track of everything we sold and of course some locals were in the bar. They must have called Papa and told him, "I don't know what she's doing but she's pouring left and right and no money's going in the till." But he had not said anything to me until later on because the next morning he was coming in and counting everything and everything was fine. They paid at the end of the shift, and we did when I worked with another bartender. We did make some good money and they tipped very well.

Papa liked the ship so much that at the end of the season Betsy, his wife, and his daughter baked a cake that looked exactly like the *Prinsendam*, it had the lights inside and everything, and brought it down for a bon voyage party. Later the *Prinsendam* had a mishap.

---

streets that it was the first local business to offer a kickback to ship staff who recommended it onboard. That seemed shocking at the time. Now it's a given than anyone who wants a piece of that pie pays a fee.

To my surprise I would learn that even visitors who seemed to suggest they were above shopping, in the end were not. A few years after starting out on the streets I began planning trips for independent travelers, people seeking an alternative to cruise ships or group bus tours. They asked for itineraries focusing on wildlife viewing, outdoor photography, local culture and history. They told me they wanted to avoid cities. So I took them at their word, sending them out of town in every possible direction, bringing them back just long enough to spend the night before catching the next ferry or flight out. I soon learned people don't always mean what they say. Even they wanted to go downtown, to shop. The U.S. travel industry says what we already knew: the most popular travel activity for American travelers is shopping.

At midnight on October 4, 1980, while traveling through the Gulf of Alaska en route to Singapore from Vancouver, B.C., fire broke out in the engine room of the Prinsendam. The Coast Guard's rescue coordination center in Juneau received the distress call and began to organize a rescue effort by air and sea. Nine hours later 20 passengers and two Air Force aviator technicians were still reported missing in one of the Prinsendam's lifeboats. Some 18 hours after the ordeal began, the Boutwell spotted a flare from the lifeboat, passengers were recovered and the rescue was over with no deaths or serious injuries. All 524 of its crew and passengers were saved due to the efforts of the U.S. Coast Guard, several other agencies and a supertanker.

Back in 1984 I couldn't imagine why any tourist would shop at a dress shop instead of a gallery or gift shop, though a friend who owned a local dress shop assured me that they did. "What kind of souvenir is that?" I'd think. Later as a tourist myself I bought a lightweight black v-neck cardigan made in Australia, from a Melbourne Target store. And I bought a black turtle-neck cropped sweater with fringe around the bottom in a small London shop after failing to pack warm enough clothing for a January theater tour. Years later they are mainstays in my wardrobe, and they never fail to conjure up warm images of those trips when I put them on.

Souvenirs, even tacky ones, are a tangible remnant of an intangible experience, explains Beverly Gordon, a professor of human ecology at the University of Wisconsin. They offer a way to hold on to where we go and what we do.

My own favorites: lava from Hawaii's Big Island, tiny rocks from the Great Wall of China, a Pepsi bottle with the label printed in Chinese, a small wine glass from Thai Airlines. In

5. A Memorable Alaskan Character

The manager of the Red Dog and I took Mary Joyce out for her birthday dinner in 1975 to the Prospector Hotel, which was known for its pepper steak and seafood. She did not tell us her age, no one knew her age. Her life story is told in *Mary Joyce: Taku to Fairbanks, 1,000 Miles by Dogteam*. When I read this book recently, I remembered when I knew her.

Mary Joyce owned the Lucky Lady Bar on South Franklin Street, living in an apartment above the bar. She would come down in the evenings about 7 p.m., have two martinis, then go up to her apartment for the night.

Before the Lucky Lady, she had the Top Hat Bar across the street and lived on Ferry Way, which was still a red light district at that time. She also owned a bar on Douglas Island. When she closed the Top Hat bar at 2 in the morning, she would shuttle her customers in a taxi to her other bar on the island which closed at 5 in the morning.

Mary was also a movie star. I'm not a movie star, but I had worked on an educational film, in helping to train potential police officers in 2011 in Aurora, CO.

Mary Joyce was a pilot. I also learned how to fly a Cessna 180, in 1976. At that time I was bartending at the Triangle Club. To this day I still have my student license. This was through the Civil Air Patrol that I had joined for a short time.

In so many ways, Mary's life and mine were similar in the things that we did. No, I never led a dog-sled team, but I had been at the Taku Lodge by the Taku Glacier, which Mary Joyce had owned at one time, for a most wonderful salmon bake.

I feel privileged to have known Mary Joyce. She is a lasting memory in my life.

retrospect a snow globe would have been better than the first two—at least I would not have desecrated the landscape or artifacts. Some years ago, one of our volunteer cruise ship greeters went aboard the ship she typically met every week and did a little shopping survey of her own. She stood by the ramp as passengers re-boarded and asked them to open their shopping bags and show her what they had purchased. Most popular, by far, was not a tee-shirt nor a refrigerator magnet. It was a condom from the Red Dog, packaged in a matchbook-style folder that proclaims "Matchless protection. You have got to be putting me on." Older travelers were buying them, giggling, and having their pictures taken not in front of the swinging doors, but by the window displaying saloon merchandise, with a sign advertising rubbers. A previous owner once told me the bar makes more money on merchandise than on drinks, though he neglected to specify which items. Now I think of the new floor constructed atop the bar as the house that rubber built.

"The street we're driving on was once under water," I continued as we drove on. "The ocean water came right up to the right-hand side of the street. As a rule of thumb, if it's flat, it's on fill."

My van started to climb where South Franklin transitioned to North Franklin.

"Now we're off fill and on bedrock," I'd say.

Even downtown, barely out of sight of their ship, someone would often ask, "How high above sea level are we?" I treated it like a serious question. Travel is disorienting, and I wasn't one to smirk at someone engaged enough to ask a question.

"On your right is the Baranof Hotel." It was named for the first governor of Russian America, Aleksandr Andreevich Baranov, who ruled with a cruel hand during 1790-1811. Why do we name buildings for people like that? At some point in the tour I'd tell them about *Ashana*, a clash of cultures novel about

Baranov and the young Tlingit woman he forced from her beloved and into his own bed. In the book there were two children—at least that much may be true; Baranof reportedly had two children by a Native woman. The story was told from the young woman's point of view, with her memories of the culture she left behind, a rare perspective in itself. I would tell the people in my van where to find the local downtown bookstore to get a copy of their own. One of my passengers, a young man from Mumbai, was so taken with the book that when we kept in touch for several years he invariably asked if the authors, husband and wife who wrote under E.P. Roesch, had written any more books. I never did find a second book; *Ashana* itself is now available only on the secondary market for as little as a penny plus shipping and handling, proof that price and value are not necessarily related.

By mid-1850s Russia wanted to sell Alaska and the United States wanted to buy. Neither cared much for Great Britain, which also showed interest in buying it. There's nothing like a common enemy to forge bonds. Sea otter pelts were no longer plentiful or profitable for Russia, and Russia's newly acquired lands in China offered better access to the Pacific Ocean and East Asia markets. They never could conquer the indigenous Tlingit Indians of Southeast Alaska. But timing wasn't right. Russia had already lost the Crimean War to Britain, France and Turkey, and the U.S. Civil War still menaced.

When the Civil War was over, with Russia the only major European power to support the Union side, it was time to consummate the deal. In 1867 the double-headed eagle, symbol of Russian America, gave way to the Stars and Stripes with 37 stars (the newest state, Nebraska, had just joined in March). It was a visionary purchase, $7.2 million or less than two cents per acre for a territory largely unknown, except of course, to the indigenous people who'd likely crossed the Bering land bridge now submerged by the Bering Sea several millennia ago.

So much history, so little time. Downtown is compact, and passed by quickly; now I was focusing on what could be seen immediately out the window.

"The Baranof was one of the nicest hotels on the West Coast when it was built in 1935." I realize now that was part of local folklore. A few people from San Francisco might differ, but no one ever challenged it. I have no idea if it was true, but I liked to think it was.

When this was a young Territory, then a young state, and most legislators left their families at home, the work of the legislative chambers spilled over into the Baranof. Legislators and lobbyists mingled in the Bubble Room, and the frontier sometimes moved in a haze of smoke and spirits.

The Baranof was freshly remodeled in 1984. On a Friday morning, April 27, on the cusp of the summer tourist season and just 12 days after my first day on the streets, a newly-fired employee lit and overturned an oil lamp in the dining room. The ensuing fire gutted the first floor, where sprinklers had been planned but not yet installed. The fire department called upon Blue's husband, an electrician with the power company, because they did not know layout of electrical switches in the newly remodeled section. Included in the $1.5 million damage were several oil paintings by Eustace Ziegler and "The Gambler" by Don Clever. Ziegler was a prolific artist, popular in Alaska and the Pacific Northwest. A trained artist (and Episcopal minister), Ziegler included people in his paintings while many artists were capturing the landscape. His bold palette knife strokes managed to be at the same time realistic and impressionistic, and fine galleries still seek his work.

Clever, born in Alberta, Canada, taught himself to paint and found his niche as a mural painter in San Francisco. His *Gambler* was reportedly painted as part of the Works Progress Administration, commonly called WPA, to provide economic relief during the Great Depression.

By coincidence, the owner of a local art gallery had imported an expert in restoration for staff training a month before the fire. When the damaged canvases were consigned to the landfill, he rushed forward to save them, calling it "Project Phoenix," new life rising from the ashes. A few paintings were damaged beyond salvage, but they were able to save several by painstakingly removing dirt and soot with long-stemmed hospital Q-tips, water and acetone. *The Gambler* alone took six months. When one painting was removed from the frame for cleaning, a second unknown painting was found on the back. The laminate was carefully split, and the result was two signed paintings. Today you can see the two rescued Zieglers in the hotel lobby, around the corner from the registration desk.

Among the lost was *Bubble Lady*, a nude surrounded by bubbles who inspired the name of a hotel bar, the Bubble Room. Heat had melted the surface. The restored "Gambler" hangs across the hall from the restored Zieglers, above the open bar still called the Bubble Room lounge.

"The hotel has just reopened," I could tell my passengers on July 6. A good part of my monologue came from reading the local newspaper and listening to the radio newscasts. Anything of wider interest was fodder for the day's narrative with my passengers. "Rebuilding cost $5 million," I reported five weeks later. And two days after that I announced, "The man who set the fire has been convicted."

---

6. Step by Step

Delivery people, from grocery to appliance stores, might charge $1 per step to carry merchandise to the front doors of downtown hillside homes accessible only by steep stairways. Boys from the grocery store would charge $1 per step to carry groceries up.

Usually I'd continue driving straight up North Franklin, which was growing more vertical by the block.

"It looks just like a New England fishing village," people would say as we drove past commercial buildings and into residential neighborhoods dating back to the mining days of the early 1900s. Victorian houses have been restored by what you might call our intelligentsia. Artists, musicians, writers, anyone who envisages a bohemian lifestyle, all gravitate downtown.

Someone would usually notice the stairways climbing the surrounding hillsides like ladders. "We have stairways that connect streets like vertical sidewalks," I'd say if someone else hadn't mentioned them first. Metal grating allows rainwater to drain away.

Like streets, the stairways have names: Carroll Way, Ewing Way, Boroff Way. The Fourth Street stairs climb 187 steps, dating back to early founding of the city in the late 1800s. Some hillside homes have front doorsteps opening onto the stairways. It helps to be fit, if not young, to call this home. Stairway people learn to shop for groceries in small quantities and they learn who their friends really are. On occasion, black bear find the stairs as handy as people do for traversing the hillside.

Eight blocks up is as high as you can drive from the waterfront, except for a single road that leads back into the Last Chance Basin and historic gold mine relics. The narrow road into the basin made it perfect for groups in small vehicles like ours, less so for busloads.

Drives back into the basin were among my favorites. It took longer and they were not part of our regular route. The basin was included on special, more leisurely tours. Though it was the equivalent of a few blocks above the city, it felt a world away. From the dock tourists could look up at the Mt. Juneau waterfall coursing the mountain's full height. Here, ensconced amid 3,500-foot peaks, its song filled their consciousness.

Devil's club grew higher than most people's heads, with dinner-plate-sized leaves shaped like maple leaves. Hermit thrush sang. Bear and mountain goats crossed a wide avalanche slope.

Blue and I led our passengers on foot past rusting rail cars and up a mountainside path to an old compressor building that houses the Last Chance Mining Museum. En route we crossed a bridge spanning Gold Creek, the stream where Juneau's founders first "found" nuggets of gold. Left on their own, Joe Juneau and Richard Harris wouldn't have looked much beyond their main passions: local women and home brew. Local Indians knew about the gold, of course, but didn't see much use for a metal too soft to be practical and too dull to be pretty. Chief Cowee of the Auk Tlingits led Juneau and Harris by the hand to the nuggets. If the Europeans were so interested, he must have thought, they may as well benefit.

After visiting the museum we lingered along the clear rushing stream. Blue and I opened aluminum thermos bottles to pour cups of the special Russian tea we'd prepared at home, fragrant with cinnamon and honey. We were ever looking to add our own twist in our tours. The sweet, sticky drink was

---

7. Teufel's Kralle (Devil's Club)

Tlingits used it to make an ointment for arthritis. It's Teufel's Kralle, in German.

Devil's Club Leaves

especially warming on a chill rainy day, but everyone agreed one cup was enough.

Traditional Russian Tea Recipe:

1 cup Tang

1/2 cup lemon-flavored instant tea

1 1/4 cups sugar

1 teaspoon cinnamon

1/4 teaspoon ground cloves

Place 2 heaping teaspoons of mix in mug; top with hot water.

Our Version of Russian Tea:

Brew tea bags or loose tea with whole cloves and stick cinnamon. Put 1 teaspoon orange marmalade and squeeze of honey in mug, top with brewed tea.

On my regular tour I would just drive North Franklin to Sixth Street, turn right and loop down on Gold Street to circle the Russian Orthodox Church, looking for a place to park so people could go inside. The Orthodox priests and monks presented the softer side of Russian occupation, expressing a genuine interest in the Natives and their culture, while the fur traders ruthlessly exploited their labor. Orthodox priests did not try to suppress Tlingit language and culture, unlike American missionaries who would follow them. So Tlingits gravitated toward the Orthodox church, where their native languages were used, and still are today.

By the mid-1880s Juneau was a new frontier town in the throes of a gold rush, and missionaries from Roman Catholic and Protestant churches soon came north. But in older neighboring Sitka and Angoon, most Tlingit had already embraced Eastern Orthodox Christianity during the Russian occupation. When the Bishop of Aleutian Islands and Alaska visited Juneau in 1892, local Tlingit leaders invited him to establish a church here. The eight-sided blue and white St. Nicholas Russian Orthodox Church, on the National Register of Historic Places, dates back to 1894. Regular services are still conducted in Russian, Tlingit and English, following the Orthodox calendar

Continuing back downhill, visitors got their first glimpse of the state capitol from the rear. The heart of government office buildings lies just three blocks inland; the capitol is on Fourth Street. The proximity is deceiving. Office workers spent their days mostly oblivious and indifferent to what was happening on the nearby waterfront. I turned right onto Fourth Street.

"This is the state capitol." I pointed to a boxy reddish brick building with four marble pillars across the front, ahead on the right. "The marble came from Prince of Wales Island near Ketchikan," I'd tell them. There is no dome, nothing particularly grand to make it stand out. Alaskan architectural preference still leans toward the basic box. When Juneau's mayor sponsored a design competition for a new capitol, architects from in and outside of Alaska responded with bold entries of futuristic glass and steel. The locals, who may or may not know a Louis Sullivan from an Eero Saarinen, clearly know what they do not like and they were unimpressed. In designs intended to reflect the sweep and character of a powerful landscape and its people, they saw a spaceship, a hard-boiled egg and a toy Slinky.

While circling through downtown, I tried to give my passengers a sense of where they had docked that day. I figured it was nearly as easy for port stops as airport terminals to blend indistinguishably together, and I was often right.

"It was the Territorial capital before Alaska became a state. It opened in 1931 as a Territorial and federal building and once held the jail and the post office."

"What is the bell in front?"

It was another frequent question. "It's a replica of the Liberty Bell," I'd explain. "Each state has one." They were distributed as part of a campaign to promote the sale of U.S. Savings Bonds. Alaska received hers in 1950, while statehood was still nearly a decade away.

The capitol only merited a few sentences from me and it doesn't fare much better in guidebooks, where editors likely assume that's not the reason most tourists head our way.

1984 was the last summer for seven years that I could point out *Nimbus*, a five-ton, 16-foot-tall metal sculpture commissioned in 1977 for the Dimond Courthouse plaza just across the street and downhill from the capitol.

Designed by New York artist Robert Murray and funded at $40,000 by the Alaska State Council on the Arts, the State Court System, and the National Endowment for the Arts, it sparked immediate controversy when it was installed in 1978.

I often saw visitors take pictures of each other with Nimbus as a backdrop or frame. Made up of curving steel planes and sharp angles, it takes on different forms depending on your direction of view.

After designing Nimbus, Murray went on to win numerous awards for large scale abstract metal sculptures throughout his native Canada and the United States. He favors painting them in bright primary colors, and one admiring biographer says he has solved the problem of sculpture in an urban environment by creating pieces strong enough to hold their own against the surrounding architecture.

That was the problem for Nimbus. It more than held its own. It was big, it was audacious, and it was a shade of green no one could wrap their mind around. Like modern architecture, contemporary art still struggles for acceptance amid what some call Alaska's "spruce and moose" genre. The Alaska State Legislature ordered removal of the sculpture in spring of 1984. By December it was banished to a state

Nimbus, now located near the Alaska State Museum

warehouse where rust eventually took hold, the smooth surface dented and the paint color that no one could name began to fade. The courthouse plaza eventually got a new sculpture, a bigger than life bronze of a brown bear fishing for salmon. *Windfall Fisherman*, by Juneau artist Skip Wallen, is a popular all-Alaskan backdrop for countless vacation photos.

In 1991, Nimbus was accessioned into the collection of the Alaska State Museum and installed, with the blessing of the artist, in a lawn off-side of the museum. It is sadly rusting and flaking around the base and dents are still visible from years spent on its side.

You can see it there today, walk through it and around it, and ponder anew the passions art can stir.

Up the hill is the Governor's Mansion, an antebellum residence for the governor and family members. Some governors have had school-aged children, one was a bachelor, some were empty-nesters. Only one sitting president, Warren G. Harding, has visited the mansion. On July 15, 1923, he drove the golden spike in the Alaska Railroad at Nenana south of Fairbanks. He traveled in Southeast Alaska the following week, and died under still questionable circumstances in San Francisco less than two weeks later. Three electoral votes don't get you much attention. Gerald Ford came for dinner when he was an ex-president, in 1989.

In 1984 Alaska's governor was Bill Sheffield. He lived in the Governor's Mansion as a bachelor and when he was out of town he freely opened second floor quarters normally off-limits as private family space. Tours by his spirited and droll housekeeper brought guaranteed laughs, and we'd include the mansion when people arranged tours well in advance and spent more time with us than the typical two and one-half hours.

"You can come back just before Christmas," I'd say on our drive-by tours. "There'll be free cookies and punch and you can shake the governor's hand." The first open house at the mansion was held on New Year's Day in 1913, and the holiday season tradition has continued every year since except for two years during World War II. The mansion staff spend fall months baking the cookies and the governor's appointed commissioners pass them out to people outside waiting in line to enter. Holiday lights outline the mansion exterior from just after Thanksgiving into January, and ribbons and boughs hang on the wrought iron fence surrounding the yard, funded by private donations.

"The mansion was built and furnished for $40,000," I'd say. It was in Governor Sheffield's term in 1983 that plumbing, heating and electrical systems were updated for $2.5 million. I'd point out the mansion's own totem pole, with its legends about the origin of man, why the tides move in and out and why there are mosquitoes. It was an interesting juxtaposition of stories, perhaps reflecting the mood during the winter of 1939-40, when it was carved by Tlingit carvers from Klukwan and Saxman as part of a Civilian Conservation Corp employment project.

Just downhill I'd drive past early 1900s homes of commercial fishermen, tiny houses with postage stamp lots. Here was a good place to point out the mini-climates and how quickly they change around mountains. Downtown hasn't been glaciated like the Mendenhall Valley nine miles away. The soil is richer with humus. It gets more direct light as the sun tracks through the sky. Downtown's annual average of 90 inches of rain and melted snow is 50 percent more abundant than in the valley, and winter temperatures are often 10 degrees warmer. Spring flowers bloom a month earlier here, and some species thrive that would barely survive in parts of the valley.

One of the houses I liked to point out had a shingled roof thick with moss, so thick that a spruce tree grew about a foot high from the spongy green carpet of growth. Yes, we lived with rain. This was tangible proof everyone could understand.

Then, a few years into my life as a tour guide, new owners moved in and installed a metal roof.

4. Out the Road

The driving loop through downtown took about 15 minutes if we didn't make any stops. Then I'd head my red van out of town, or what we call "out the road." I had a compass attached to the windshield, just above the rear view mirror, and pinned a small black ball compass to my left breast pocket.

People laughed. "Don't you know where you're going?" they'd ask.

Directions are deceptive when you're winding around mountains. They'd think surely they were facing east, when it was due north. It made for conversation, and was another small way I tried to anchor them with a sense of where they were.

We were driving what felt as if it should be north, but was actually northwest and even west. I often took the old Glacier Highway, a bench road overlooking the main Egan Expressway and once the only road out of town. We drove past houses, which always interested people, past the high school, past a couple of early bed & breakfast homes before merging onto the Egan Expressway in one and one-half miles. I liked it because I could drive slower, giving me more time to point out the succession of wildflowers coming into bloom.

Each year I noted on a spiral notebook calendar the first sighting of each variety of wildflower, where it bloomed, and the easiest and best place to photograph it. Loren Eiseley, an anthropologist, science writer and ecologist, wrote an essay he entitled *How Flowers Changed the World*. He called the emergence of flowering plants late in the Age of Reptiles a "soundless, violent explosion." As they spread their encased seeds far and wide, they created food for all kinds of new creatures both great and small.

My own take was less scientific. I treasured flowers for the way they defined the seasons and colored our lives.

First to appear, in early April, is the showy skunk cabbage. A single spike of tiny green flowers, both male and female, is cupped by a large curved bracket, called a spathe, the color of butter. Bear emerging from dens about the same time eat the roots as a laxative; deer nibble on the flowers while still at lower elevations, before melting snow allows them to retreat upward to summer feeding grounds.

Blue called them her tulips. As a newcomer to Juneau she picked the striking flowers and put them in a vase. The strong odor that inspired their name soon filled her house. It's hard for a flower with such an unfortunate name and fragrance to garner the respect it deserves. Skunk cabbage is like a clean-lined contemporary sculpture, dramatic, decidedly phallic, and no less sensual than Edward Weston's "Pepper, 1930" or Georgia O'Keeffe's "Calla Lily Turned Away."

I knew where they grew at the end of old Glacier Highway, near an easy out-of-the-way place to park the van. By the time most visitors arrive, the flowers have been eaten or fallen away, but the leaves continue to grow through the summer. The largest leaves of any native plant, they can reach as much as 50 inches long and 30 inches wide. For Tlingits they were better than aluminum foil, perfect for wrapping a whole salmon baking in a fire.

Skunk Cabbage

A patch of forget-me-nots, our state flower, blossomed in the same area. They grew in tandem with buttercups that echoed the bright yellow center of the forget-me-nots. It made for a nice photo composition. In a place where big is the norm, people seemed surprised that the state flower was so small. The Territorial legislature adopted it in 1917, perhaps because it grows from southern southeast Alaska to the Arctic Coast and west to the Aleutians. Here it blooms all summer. As a tour guide I liked things like that, predictable and dependable.

This is a linear town, with one main highway linking the downtown center with the residential Mendenhall Valley, Juneau's bedroom, its biggest housing area and birthplace of the local commute. Most of our 30,000 residents of working age drive between valley home and downtown office each weekday. There's no urban sprawl downtown; the 3,500-foot mountains behind the waterfront see to that. Juneau's sprawl is nine miles away, where the mountains yield to a broad valley conveniently carved by the Mendenhall Glacier that still lingers at its head. As the glacier retreated back into the valley it carved, it left rare flat land easy to tame into somewhat typical suburban housing developments.

I'd already driven this highway from my home in the valley to the dock, noting the tides, eagles, wildflowers on the way in. I watched the weather, the way clouds were hanging, the lighting for photography, whether rain meant less time outside the van. When clouds were so low that helicopter glacier landing tours were cancelled, it meant more business for shops in town and more potential customers for sightseeing businesses like mine. On a good day I'd make two round trips on this road before heading home again in late afternoon.

The road heading out of town hugs the shore of Gastineau Channel on the left and skirts mountains to the right. Soon after merging onto the expressway I'd point out our hospital on a hill to the right, adding that I hoped they wouldn't need its services. It was a small way of reassuring them they were somewhere safe, somewhere with the amenities they knew back home. I didn't add that a cruise ship schedule calendar hung in the emergency room, just as it did on my refrigerator at home, nor that we heard the hospital derived about a quarter of its annual revenue from summer visitors. In the 1980s most cruise ship passengers were seniors, and an ambulance pulling up to the dock was not uncommon. For a few it would be their last journey. Passengers have gotten younger since then, with more active shore excursions and concerted wooing by cruise lines. But I suspect the calendar still hangs there.

Just past the intersection to the hospital, the Chilkat Mountains come into view, filling the horizon with a fluorescent white. Thanks to their proximity to the vast ice of Glacier Bay, the Chilkats keep their snow cover year around, and on a clear day they draw you into themselves.

"On the other side of the mountains is Glacier Bay," I'd say, knowing that most of my cruise ship passengers would be there within a day or two. "On this side of the mountains is Lynn Canal, the major waterway linking Juneau to Haines and Skagway. The Chilkat Mountains form a wall between the two."

Lynn Canal is the marine link via Alaska Marine Highway between Juneau and Miami, or San Francisco or St. Louis.

I'd tell them they were on the mainland, firmly attached to the rest of North America. About this point someone would say, "I heard you can't drive here."

It was a frequent comment that usually ended with an unspoken question: "How can you stand to live somewhere so isolated?"

People were shocked. Shocked! What does it mean, isolated? Isolated from whom? Isolated from what? It was time for one of my favorite stories.

"Isolation is a state of mind," I'd start out. One day a momentous calamity–it doesn't matter what it was–brought

56

television news crews to rural Nova Scotia, a place remote by many standards. A local woman, who'd never traveled far from her home, listened quietly as one TV reporter regaled her with stories of the great Eastern seaboard. He told her of the millions of people living in an arc from Boston to New York City to Washington D.C. She paused, then asked "Why would all those people want to live so far away from everything?"

"That's how we feel," I'd say, though in retrospect it was presumptuous to lay this sentiment on my fellow Juneau residents who are, per capita, among the most traveled people I've encountered. "Why would you want to leave here?"

They'd exchange knowing smiles at the provincialism of their driver and her little world.

So what if you can't drive here, I thought to myself. What is this fixation with the automobile anyhow? It has ruined cities and neighborhoods. Ribbons of concrete. Cloverleaves. What pastoral, romantic names for the Gordian knots we've created in the name of freedom of the road. Freedom to spend hours of quality time hermetically sealed in a vehicle, seething at faceless nameless people around you? Now that's isolation. Commuting two hours, anywhere, so you can "live" in the country—that's shocking. There are urban centers so clogged with cars that weather or human disasters can paralyze them in less time than it takes get a pizza delivered. Can you drive to Great Britain? No, you take a plane or a boat or the Chunnel. But you can't drive. And most everybody arrives by air, same as here.

I'd start scanning trees for eagles, grateful for creatures of habit. They tend to choose the same perch every year, moving as their food supply, primarily salmon, changes location. Like the forget-me-nots, they made my job easier. Eagles hadn't yet begun their remarkable comeback in other states, and seeing eagles was near the top of every visitor's wish list. I was able to produce eagles with a predictability that amazed visitors.

One day my passengers spanned three generations, a grandmother, a mother, and a boy I judged to be about 10. I'd been contracted in advance to provide a private tour, and picked them up at a downtown hotel. They had crisscrossed the state by air several times, flown to the Russian Far East and landed in Juneau, their last stop. The boy seemed a bit glazed and over-sated by it all. He asked only one thing of this day—to see a bald eagle. We looked in all the reliable spots and drove to out-of-the-way places. I scanned tree tops and water's edge. It was the only day in my memory I could not bring forth the sighting of an eagle. A little boy had one simple wish and I failed him.

The expressway continued past Lemon Creek Valley, smaller than the Mendenhall Valley but with Thunder Mountain as a shared valley wall. There are smaller hanging glaciers at the valley head, some homes and commerce. A brewery set up home here in 1986, using a recipe dating back to 1899, and winning national and international taste tests every year since. Now the valley hosts big box stores, rental storage units, small businesses, a maximum security prison and the local police station. Looking up, beyond eye level, you can see how lovely this place once was.

Sometimes I'd take the loop road through Lemon Creek, if I hadn't already found good eagle sightings. The birds were drawn by the land fill, but often perched on spruce overlooking a church. "These are the Mormon eagles," I'd say, referring to the church beneath their trees. "They're of better character than the junkyard eagles." People laughed, but with no likely food supply at the church you knew they were all birds of a feather.

Our drive on the expressway out of town continued past the Mendenhall Wetlands, stretching nine miles along the channel. Wetlands are finally getting their due. Creating the Mendenhall Wetlands State Game Refuge back in 1976 took a decade of prodding by local citizens. It's still more symbolic than protective, but it's a start. Now it's more common knowledge that wetlands have big boots to fill. Quietly, unassumingly, they go about absorbing floodwaters, filtering runoff, absorbing the forces of wind and tides as well as providing food and habitat for everything from tiny worms and grasses to birds on the move. Still they're too often drained for construction that turns out to be–surprise!–built in a floodplain.

My passengers would hear how the saltwater Mendenhall Wetlands are one of three major stopovers for migrating birds traversing the Pacific Flyway between Arctic nesting grounds and winter homes in California and western Mexico. The first stopover, south of here, is the Stikine Flats near Wrangell. The third is the Copper River Delta off the Gulf of Alaska near Cordova. Wrangell and Cordova weren't regular port calls for big cruise ships, so this was the travelers' chance to see one of the three areas critical for migratory birds.

Identifying birds beyond the most familiar of species was not one of my strong suits, but that didn't dampen my enthusiasm for urging others to take up bird watching. Today I'd tell visitors a total of 230 species were documented in the Mendenhall Wetlands from 1986 to 2002, more than three-quarters of all species seen in the entire Juneau area.

None of my passengers escaped hearing how the 4,500-acre wetlands are a major destination for even hard-core birders, who lead weekly spring migration bird walks for Juneau Audubon Society mid-April into June. During peak migration, April and May, more than 16,000 individual birds can stop by on a single day: Canada Goose, Mallard, Surf Scoter, Ruddy Turnstone, Surfbird, Western Sandpiper, Bonaparte's Gull, Mew Gull, Glaucous-winged Gull, Northwestern Crow to name a few. Some species turn up over a thousand at a time. When the Juneau airport runway came into view from the expressway I'd talk about the dike trail that parallels the runway on the other side. It was my own introduction to that trail that eventually led me to the driver's seat in this van.

Only on rare occasions could I, in those early years, coax travelers to take time from more familiar attractions to walk the trail during their brief time in port. When I succeeded, we went not so much for birds, who were mostly absent during summer travel season, but for the wildflowers. In July the path is lined with stalks of fireweed, my personal favorite. The plant came by its common name as one of the first flowers to revegetate land burned by forest fires, and it's also found on land newly bared by retreating glaciers. It's one of the pioneer species, taking root in poor soil, fixing nitrogen and making way for other plants. I loved its fuchsia brilliance in our green forest, the way it glowed especially on rainy days, how you could hear the wing beats as Rufous Hummingbirds zoomed from blossom to blossom.

If the tide was in as we continued to skirt the channel on our drive out of town, people asked if their ship would come this way when they sailed from Juneau. If the tide was out people looked out on a grassy meadow and asked why no one had built there. Either way, it was a cue to talk about the tides, how they swung between low and high every 6½ hours. Around Juneau extreme high tides reach about plus-20 feet, lowest of the low tides drop to minus-4 feet, a total range of 24 vertical feet. The actual range varies every day.

"At low tide it's like someone pulled the plug on the bath water," I'd say. When we retraced our route along the expressway an hour later I'd point out a noticeable difference in the water level.

"Our ship is sinking," a distraught woman once told Blue as the tide moved out at the city dock. With a likely change of 10 to 12 vertical feet in water level during port call, I could understand how someone might think that. A ship arriving on high tide may force passengers to navigate a steep ramp down to dock level. As the tide falls, the ramp to reboard could be nearly level.

I'd hand a small tide table booklet to the passenger seated across from me, paper-clipped to open to Juneau and the current month, and ask them when high and low tides would occur on that day. For most it was the first time they'd seen a tide table, and I'd explain how it listed times and levels for low and high tides on every day of the year. Some seemed genuinely intrigued, and I'd tell them they could get their own tide table free at a local bank or hardware store.

Canada's Bay of Fundy between New Brunswick and Nova Scotia claims the greatest tidal range with a change of up to 50 feet and 100 billion tons of seawater in one day. Cook Inlet, a 180-mile lance thrust into the underbelly of Southcentral Alaska, has extreme tidal ranges of more than 35 feet.

While ours are not that dramatic, I had our own story of tides and storms generating a storm surge on Thanksgiving Day of 1984.

"It was the day a lot of turkeys didn't finish roasting."

The high tide was about 20 feet, the wind gusts about 90 miles per hour. The sea drove inland, washing out part of the Marine Park dock and lapping across our lone waterfront highway near downtown. Power lines and trees toppled, boats sank, airplanes flipped.

I always liked telling stories you'd know firsthand only as a year-round resident.

And I'd tell people about locals who harvest and cook clams during the minus tides and about the tingle test.

"They'll give a small bite to one person to eat, and watch to see if they start tingling," I'd say.

"If they don't tingle, the clams are safe." What makes clams less than safe is the presence of PSP, or paralytic shellfish poisoning. One early symptom is tingling in the lips, tongue, fingers and toes. Should nausea, dizziness, vomiting or diarrhea occur there's no antidote short of a trip to a nearby hospital, preferably within minutes. If enough toxin is ingested it can paralyze muscles that control breathing. Shellfish harvested for retail sales in Alaska and elsewhere are tested for safety in advance, but there's no do-it-yourself safety test, and a beach clam cookout with friends or family could end up as something more than the party you'd planned.

PSP occurs when toxins concentrate in clams and oysters feeding on microscopic algae. As Captain George Vancouver was exploring the waters around Vancouver Island and Puget Sound in 1793, he reported at least four crewmen fell ill after eating mussels for breakfast; one died. Six years later, a large party of Aleut hunters under the command of Aleksandr Baranov left Sitka Island by skin boats bound for Kodiak. They

8. Thanksgiving on a Charcoal Grill

That Thanksgiving we had such high Taku winds, they were measured at 200 knots per hour. And of course everybody in town had their turkey ready to stick in the oven but when the power went off they couldn't get the turkey going. So my husband Jerry had to go out with the crew and help remove trees that had fallen over houses. He was superintendent for a power company from Seattle, it was Service Electric. Thankfully nobody was hurt but they worked all through that night, through the next day, and they had to have some food. So we were making sandwiches and we made some kind of a soup and took that out to the crew and that got them through. It was really something and then they announced, "Oh don't everybody turn on your oven at once" and the thing goes out again. So we had auxiliary power, but it wasn't enough for a big load like this. Eventually the turkeys were cooked but it was after Thanksgiving.

dined on small black mussels on an overnight stop at Khutznov Strait. Within two minutes half the party felt nauseated and had dry throats, according to Baranov's account. By the end of two hours, about a hundred had died. Those who survived reportedly took a mixture of gunpowder, tobacco and spirits to make themselves throw up. Khutznov Strait is now called Peril Strait.

Talking fast now, with so much still to say about the channel paralleling the expressway, I moved to the theory of isostatic rebound. I talked about it as though it was an unchallenged given, though it's now clear not everyone subscribes to it.

"It's a fancy term for describing how the ground is slowly rising after glaciers retreated," I'd say. Tons of ice were a mighty burden upon the land that is now set free. "The

---

The crews had to secure everything, remove debris. We had a charcoal grill, put the pot on it; we cooked on the porch. It was just something we threw together, like a vegetable, whatever we had. Sandwiches we made from whatever we had, my own refrigerator and everyone else helped. The wives, the girl friends, we all pulled together. Some other people, too. That's just the great thing about Juneau. When somebody needs something you don't even have to say anything. People are pulling together and they help each other and that's exactly what that was all about.

The phones were out too so we had to actually find the crews. We just drove around looking for them. You saw somebody, you asked "Did you see so and so?"

"Oh yeah, he's over here, he's over there." If you found one, you found them all. They had their radios so they could talk to each other.

Mendenhall Refuge is rising about six-tenths of an inch a year."
When we drove across milky Lemon Creek I'd point to the
glacial streams and their role in rising land levels. As silt-laden
streams empty into saltwater they drop their burden of rock
ground fine as face powder. "The channel was dredged in the
1950s to allow boats to get through," I said, "but it filled right
back up again." At least once a summer an inexperienced or
careless mariner would strand a small boat on a sand bar, and
have to wait for a tide high enough to set it free. Only the
smallest of boats can navigate this stretch of the channel, and
only on high tides. Other vessels traverse the deep waters of
Stephens Passage on the other side of Douglas Island.

While other coastal cities now stare down rising water levels
brought on by global warming, our isostatic rebound is
expected to safely keep us high enough to gain ground, or at
least tread water.

There was usually some point during the tour with fewer
sights to describe out the window, leaving more time for telling
longer and more complicated stories. Many passengers had at
least heard of the long-running issue of moving the capital
from Juneau to the population, economic and political center in
Southcentral Alaska. Some would ask outright: "Do you think
the capital will move out of Juneau?" This was a good place to
talk about it.

When the Territorial capital moved 120 miles east to Juneau
from the Russian America capital of Sitka in 1906, Juneau was
the center of the action. Sitka's fortunes had gone down with
the decline of whaling and fur trading, and Juneau had an
established town site growing around dozens of gold mines up
and down the coastal gold belt. In Skagway, 90 miles up Lynn
Canal, the infamous con man Soapy Smith lay in his grave, and
the narrow gauge White Pass railway connected Skagway with
gold strikes in Canada's Yukon that were already fading into
history.

Fairbanks, now Alaska's second largest city and service center for the vast Interior, was just developing after gold was found nearby in 1902, though it soon surpassed Juneau in size. The tent city that grew around construction of the Alaska Railroad and would grow into our largest city, Anchorage, was still nine years in the future.

Over Sitka's objections, no doubt, a desk and file drawers were moved to Juneau and it became the new capital. Proposed future moves would not be so simple.

I'd been in all these towns myself, and saw no reason not to pass on my opinions of each. "All our cities started at different times for different reasons," I'd say, "and each has its own unique personality." I also knew that many of these people would set foot in these communities before returning home, and I was careful not to say anything I wouldn't want repeated. In Juneau we needed our friends around the state.

As Anchorage boomed in World War II and the aftermath, the publisher of that city's major newspaper was an unabashed supporter of statehood for Alaska and of moving the capital to the new population center of the state. He had the will and the platform to run a steady stream of news stories and editorials on both issues. Did my passengers care? Well, it mattered a lot to me and they'd brought it up.

By 1984 we'd already voted on the capital move at least eight times. In 1954, a measure was passed to move the capital north, but at least 30 miles from both Anchorage and Fairbanks. Neither of those cities wanted to cede too much power to the other, and votes from both were needed to wrest it from Juneau. Propositions in 1960 and 1962 to relocate closer to Anchorage, (but not too close), both failed.

"If you don't like the answer, you ask the question again," I'd say. People could relate; in that sense politics are the same everywhere. In 1974, voters said yes to an initiative calling for construction of a new capital city at one of two or three sites nominated by a committee appointed by the Governor, with final selection to be made in a general election.

"When supporters of the move came down to Juneau on state business, they weren't the first ones served in local coffee shops," I'd tell them. There were rumors some waitresses refused to serve the most outspoken move advocates at all, while nervous local politicians were urging utmost courtesy to all visitors lest we justify taking away 80 percent of our local employment. Juneau's powerful senior senator was also adding a sentence here and there to appropriations bills.

"This four-lane highway is one result of that struggle," I'd say. Another was a new state court house and a new state office building downtown. If you invested a lot of money in pouring concrete in the capital, it would be harder to justify leaving it all behind, I'd explain. A downtown adjunct to the University of Alaska campus here bears the senator's name: the Bill Ray Center.

Two years later, when the capital site selection committee set out three possible sites, the largest number of votes went to Willow, the closest to Anchorage and abuzz with land sales and swaps. Plans called for a new capital in the wilderness, "like Canberra in Australia or Brasilia in Brazil," I'd say. Our senior senator was still at work. In 1978, a month after my husband and I moved to Juneau from Anchorage and agonized over purchasing a house amid such uncertainty, a ballot initiative required that all costs of capital relocation be determined and approved by a majority of voters before any money could be spent on the move. Every imaginable expense was packed into the proposition: moving personnel and offices; building, furnishing and financing a new capital with facilities equal to those in Juneau; and compensating for social, economic and environmental impacts to present and future location sites. Voters said "yes" to the move, "no" to the price tag calculated at $966,000,000.

Move proponents charged the price was artificially inflated. In 1982 they came up with a $2.8 million no-frills capital move to Willow. Tensions ran high between regions of the state, and those on the forefront of keeping the capital in Juneau knew they would not always be welcome in other parts of the state. They also knew that as Anchorage continued to grow as the political, economic and service center of the state, every other community was anxious to rein it in, not add to its power base. The people of Juneau breathed in and out with one breath, held hands on election night and let out a collective sigh when the measure was defeated.

I was in election central in an Anchorage hotel on election night, but even from there I was inhaling Juneau's oxygen. When I returned a day later, bells were ringing out, people had lit holiday lights early, and the relief was palpable.

People from other states saw the logic in moving the capital from this town to the center of the state's population. I voted for it myself in 1974 as a resident of Anchorage, and I picked the Willow site in 1976. Now I lived in Juneau, and stressed about my own house and the specter of closing the plant so to speak, of losing the assembly line that tears through many company towns. People who studied such things estimated 80 percent of Juneau's economy was tied to its role as state capital. And everyone could identify with wanting to protect their home.

My first stop after leaving downtown and heading "out the road," as Juneau residents call it, was usually Brotherhood Park.

I knew our real destination, the reason people climbed into my van, was the Mendenhall Glacier. Even so, I wanted to lead up to it, to approach it obliquely and include other attractions en route. You shouldn't just drive straight up to something so defining. I wanted to build anticipation, show it from many angles before approaching it as closely as possible by vehicle and then by foot.

"This is one of my favorite photo stops," I'd say as I pulled into the parking lot next to Brotherhood Bridge. The bridge spans the Mendenhall River, a river gray with silt that drains from the lake in front of the glacier. It's about four miles from the glacier, and between here and there are numerous subdivisions, my own included. But it is so well sited you see none of that. There's just a meadow filled with wildflowers in the foreground, and glacier and mountains in the background. There were plans to build a road and subdivisions here at one time, I'd say, but wiser heads prevailed and preserved this view.

"From here you can get a real sense of how ice flows between the mountains just like a river." I usually prefaced that with "We'll get closer than this, but. . . ." One day I either forgot the preface, or a passenger failed to hear me. He bolted from my van and began running through the meadow toward the glacier; the others soon followed. I came along behind, wondering what they found so compelling. It struck me as a little odd until I realized they thought this was our glacier stop, as close as they would get, and they were determined to shorten as much as possible the gap between themselves and the glacier. I learned that distant vistas, no matter how panoramic, are no match for seeing something up close. The big picture, I realized, was no substitute for the close up.

---

9. Fireweed

Fireweed, with your purple coat,
How we like to see you arrive and hate to see you go.
When you go, fall is here and nature braces itself for another season of color
But for now the fragrances and colors enhance our senses,
which make us feel so alive.

When we first started including Brotherhood Park on our tours, Blue and I had it to ourselves. Buses and taxis drove on by. Today it is a regular stop. Next to images of Denali and calving glaciers, photos from this very spot are probably the most widely used in calendars and promotional brochures. Look for a glacier in the upper middle, backed by jagged mountains, and a meadow filled with fuchsia fireweed in the foreground. That's the view from Brotherhood Park.

There was one more stop before we came to the glacier visitor center: a small log chapel. Self-proclaimed veterans of European ABC tours, (another blasted church), were noticeably unenthused when I announced yet another stop, and a church at that, before the main event. I knew to bide my time. Whenever possible I tried to reach the chapel between buses, and couldn't help gloating when I succeeded. Some things are more powerful experienced in a small group, and this was one of them. I'd park the van, point out the larger chapel used for most services, and usher my passengers through the door of the smaller log structure. Then I'd stand aside. They'd look at the altar and gasp. Behind the simple altar, where churches typically have stained glass, large clear windows look out on thick spruce, Auke Lake and yet another view of the glacier.

First they'd look in silence. Then nearly always someone would ask "How could a minister compete with that?" And someone else would say "The real sermon is outside the window."

A greeter from the congregation was usually present to tell the story of the little chapel; I also filled in some details. For many years churches in Alaska were operated as missions, as most local congregations were too small to support a church. Missionaries, beginning with S. Hall Young in Wrangell in the 1880s, were expected to send reports and travel back home to solicit funds. An East Coast woman was moved to support work of the Presbytery in Alaska, sold a diamond necklace and donated the proceeds that became seed money for this chapel. It was built by volunteers in the mid-1950s of Sitka spruce logged from nearby mountains, and furnished with pews made in a plywood factory then operating in Juneau. Spaces between the logs were chinked with gypsum, and the whole was sealed with coats of varnish used for wooden boats.

My most memorable visit to the chapel was with two middle-age sisters traveling with their husbands. They were Jewish, they said, as were many of my passengers. One sister had lost her eyesight in her early 20s. She gently ran her hand

---

10. Seeing Through Other Eyes

One time I had a group, picked them up from the cruise ship, and a lady said to me, "Can you take my family?" By that time I had a van, and it was 12-passenger. "My mother she is handicapped."

"That's okay," I said. "I'll put her in the front." She says "okay." So everyone else piled in and I was giving the tour on the way to the glacier. I'd helped this lady into the van. I said "Are you comfortable?"

"Yes, I am." I didn't see a cane or anything. I thought boy, she's pulling a fast one, just wants to sit in the front seat. As I was giving the tour, we had a beautiful day, the sun was shining and as I approached the glacier I said, "Do you see the glacier? It looks beautiful today." And then she touched my hand and she said, "Honey, I see it through your eyes for I'm blind." And I felt I was going to wilt because I had thought, "well where's she handicapped? She can move and do everything else." I did not know she was blind. So that reminds you not to take everything at face value. When she said "Honey, I see it through your eyes" I felt like crying, but I didn't dare because I had to keep driving, watch the road."

over the smooth grain of the altar as the sighted sister described it in eloquent detail. She smiled and nodded as her sister described the scene outside the window, framed by wood in the shape of a cross. Later, at the glacier, the blind woman took deep breaths and exclaimed her pleasure in the clean fresh air. In that day I felt she "saw" more of the chapel and glacier than most sighted visitors.

Most days I felt I surely had the best passengers in town— they were interested, responsive, and full of questions. But sometimes I just wanted to cry out, "Stop. Look. Really look and feel."

Now and then I'd quote Joseph Wood Krutch: "The rare moment is not the moment when there is something worth looking at but the moment when we are capable of seeing."

Helen Keller pinpointed our general failure to pay attention in her *Atlantic Monthly* essay in 1933, "Three Days to See."

"Those who have never suffered impairment of sight or hearing seldom make the fullest use of these blessed faculties. Their eyes and ears take in all sights and sounds hazily, without concentration and with little appreciation," she wrote. Like my blind passenger, Helen Keller saw by passing her hands lovingly over the world around her.

Leaving the chapel, we drove past the small campus of the University of Alaska Southeast, where classrooms look out on Auke Lake. I'd tease passengers about sending their young people to school here; all recoiled at the notion of giving them up to such a faraway place as my own family had done. This is a white collar town, and many of the students were professionals continuing their studies at night.

From campus we turned right onto the Back Loop Road, threading through the Mendenhall Valley. We'd cross the Mendenhall River again. The upper river is a tumbling turgid mass in mid-summer when snowmelt is highest. I'd drive slowly across the bridge when we saw rubber rafts bouncing on the river on a shore excursion sold aboard ships. At lowest water level in early spring the river is mostly bare rock.

We were driving straight toward Thunder Mountain by now, a good time to point out avalanche chutes extending from tree line down to the base. It was easy to point them out—the shrubby growth was a brighter green amid the deep green Sitka spruce and western hemlock.

"That's where the snow slides down every year, and the trees don't have a chance to grow. The mountain got its name from the sound of the avalanches thundering down." I'd add this mountain was the source of spruce trees used in building the log chapel we'd just left and that on spring days I could hear avalanches rumbling in my living room.

When the Back Loop road ended at a T, I'd turn left at the stop sign.

"At one time the face of the glacier came down this far," I'd say as we rounded the corner. As we drove closer to the glacier

---

11. They Talked and Talked

One time I had another group, I'm giving the tour about the history of Juneau, the gold and we were also approaching the glacier and I told them to watch out for bears and what to do; retreat very slowly, you can use the pepper spray. And as I was talking about the glacier and the bears, they were just talking among each other about stuff, this neighbor here and they did this and they did that. And I stopped talking and they looked at me and one fellow said, "Well, about the bear?" I was tired of their talking, I'd about had it.

"You know, when you approach a bear," I said, "you put your head between your legs and you kiss your ass good-bye." Silence followed for the rest of the trip.

72

I'd point out how the conifers got smaller and the willow and alder got bigger and bushier.

I'd talk about plant succession. When a glacier retreats, new land is exposed for the first time in hundreds of years, I'd explain. Plants begin to re-vegetate a barren landscape in predetermined order. First Bull's-eye and Map lichens take hold on rocks, slowly breaking down rock and absorbing nitrogen from the air. As rocks develop cracks, minerals from lichens create a tiny foothold for mosses, small willows, dwarf fireweed.

Gradually lupine takes root in nutrient-poor soil that was ground up and then discarded by retreating glaciers. Its assignment is to fix nitrogen in the soil and prepare it for other plants. In late May lupine buds are still covered by a gauzy film, a gift waiting to be opened. I'd make a note that within a week flowers should cover the erect spike, in an intense shade not quite purple, but not just blue either.

"They look just like the Texas Bluebonnets," visitors from that state often commented. Our particular species is Nootka Lupine; theirs is native only to Texas. The delicate finger-like leaves often cup a single drop of water after rain, glistening with the splendor of a fine-cut diamond. It was one of the photo ops I liked to point out on rainy days.

Sitka Alder, then gradually Sitka spruce and western hemlock follow in the rebirth of the forest. At first Sitka spruce dominate, but as they grow and create their own shade, they block the very sunlight they need to thrive. Over time the western hemlock takes the lead, accounting for about 70 percent of a mature forest.

A mature old growth forest is made up of trees of varying size and age and a complex understory of vegetation that can sustain diverse wildlife. Beginning from bare rock or cleared land, it can take up to 350 years to grow, I'd say. It was a nod to the ongoing controversy over clear-cutting in the Tongass

National Forest that makes up Southeast Alaska. I wanted to make sure they knew the stakes.

"This is your forest," I'd say, encouraging them to contact their representatives in Congress if they had opinions on management of the nation's largest national forest.

More than a million acres of trees have been clear-cut since the first pulp mill opened in 1954. Much of the old growth forest has been felled. Sitka spruce, the state tree, can grow as tall as a 25-story building, with a trunk 10 feet across and a life span of 500 to 700 years. If you'd come here before widespread logging you could have readily found yourself in the company of a tree that began as seedling when Johannes Gutenberg invented movable type printing or Leonardo da Vinci painted the Mona Lisa, or a million workers were laboring on the Forbidden City in Beijing. Now only small scattered stands of old growth are left.

"Where's the rainforest?" someone often asked.

"It's all around us," I'd say, careful not to imply any question was silly. No one should be embarrassed by an honest question, especially on vacation.

What makes a temperate rainforest? Abundant precipitation, moderate temperatures year-round, dense vegetation.

By now conversion inside my van had ended. Time for talking was over. The main event, the glacier came into view ahead, and it was all that mattered.

5. Driving to Super Bear

I called it our obligatory glacier.

"No one who comes to Juneau is allowed to leave without seeing the glacier," I'd say well before it came into view. Business travelers, family visitors, tourists, visiting artists and musicians all come to gaze upon the Mendenhall Glacier. One grocery store three miles away offers views of its 5,000-foot backdrop from round tables where customers can take a break with designer coffee and a muffin or fruit salad from the deli. Another grocer has similar views from its check-out stands.

Most towns have something defining like that, something so familiar you only need a word or two and every local knows exactly what you mean. In Anchorage it is simply "the mountain." Everyone knows you mean Denali, or Mt. McKinley, 250 miles to the north. On rare clear days people say "Did you see the mountain?" It doesn't matter if you've lived there 30 years or are visiting for a day. The mountain will be acknowledged. When I parked across the river and walked the Wabasha Street bridge to my first job in downtown St. Paul, Minnesota, no one asked which river. The Mississippi needed no explanation.

75

The Mendenhall Glacier is one of 38 large glaciers that flow from the Juneau Icefield, the fifth largest icefield in the Western Hemisphere. Our glacier is not the biggest, but it is the best known because we built a city nearby. The Juneau Icefield stretches from the Taku River about 18 miles southeast of Juneau to Skagway 90 miles north and from Juneau across the Coast Mountains to Atlin, B.C. It's a 1,500-square-mile mosaic of ice and snow.

Mendenhall Lake creates a moat between the face of the glacier and the visitor center and parking lot. The near edge of the parking lot was about a half-mile from the face of the glacier when I started taking visitors there. Distances are hard to judge around mountains without a reference marker, and few people came close to guessing it. "In the 1940s the face of the glacier reached where we're standing now," I'd say. It was a benchmark well within their lifetimes. The lake first appears on maps in 1909, but it did not begin to expand rapidly until the 1940s. During the Little Ice Age, in the 16th to 19th centuries, this glacier extended about two and one-half miles down valley, well over the lot I called home.

"The glacier is retreating 30 to 50 feet a year. It's about 13 miles long from where it first starts up on the ice cap down to the face," I'd continue. "From here we can see only three to four miles of that length."

My passengers climbed out of the van, cameras in hand, purses on arms. They stood on the sidewalk facing the glacier and paused in silence, reaching for words. Trying to wrap their thoughts around it, someone would eventually say "It's awesome" with a touch of satisfaction that at last they alone had found the perfect description for the scene before them.

"Here's the photo for your next Christmas card," I'd tell them as I snapped their pictures facing me with the glacier in the background. The people back home probably wouldn't believe them, I'd caution. It's a setting more believable as a painted backdrop, a Thomas Kinkade painting, than as something real.

A visitor center, the first constructed in a U.S. National Forest, was built into a rocky outcrop in 1962. A cozy stone fireplace and an arc of picture windows overlooking the glacier made it a magnet for visitors and locals alike. When the center was remodeled and expanded with new exhibits in 1999, it retained an organic flavor that suits its site. In the late 1980s a roofed pavilion was added, jutting toward the glacier from the parking lot. I immediately disliked this intrusion into the sidewalk panorama. What was the point? "Isn't something worth looking at without having to construct an edifice to validate it?" I'd think. "Well, maybe if it's raining," I conceded. But over time I couldn't deny people instinctively headed into the shelter in all weather, though the glacier is just as visible from the sidewalk.

Since then the three-tiered concrete and stone edifice has been the site of weddings, photo workshops, school outings, Tlingit dances, award ceremonies, and an annual Easter sunrise service. It holds tripods for photographers and people posing for outdoor portraits.

We humans seem to like the sense of order and scale that frames and walls afford. Japanese gardens frame scenes with high branching trees, gaps in hedges, even windows. American landscapers create a sense of enclosure with walls of shrubs, stones, gates and arches. Over time I've grudgingly come to see its worth and even appreciate its natural design of native stone.

"Where does the waterfall go?"

Visitors asked Blue and me that every day in 1984. A wide swath of water cascaded down bare rocks on the right-hand side, then mysteriously disappeared behind a 300-foot high wall of glacier ice. So deep and cavernous was the glacier that it absorbed the great surge without so much as a tell-tale ripple in the lake at the base. "The Nugget Creek waterfall was diverted and harnessed to power a nearby gold mine in the early 1900s; that's why it runs so full," I'd say. In mid-summer, after heavy rains, it became a screaming torrent.

Back in 1984, geologist Dr. Maynard Miller was leading student research atop the Juneau Icefield as he had done for the last 38 of his 63 years.

Dr. Miller first traveled north at the beginning of the Cold War, partly because the Navy wanted more information on the Arctic for everything from waging conventional war against Russia to designing nuclear submarines under polar ice. He soon recognized the Juneau Icefield as an incredible biographer of climactic change, and founded the Juneau Icefield Research Program. He saw that the icefield taught things you couldn't learn anywhere else about the intensity and acceleration of changes due to what we now call global warming.

Though it's just above our heads, the Juneau Icefield is mostly visible from the air unless you happen to be Dr. Miller or one of his students. In eight weeks students earn college credits for scientific study atop ice and on nunataks, the jagged mountaintops above the reach of glacial erosion. They bore holes into packed layers of snow and descend into crevasses to collect core samples that help determine annual snowfall and sediments over the course of a century. They make depth soundings, learn to read the ice like a library text book and with support of some 15 permanent icefield camps, traverse 150 miles from Juneau to Atlin Lake in northern British Columbia with skis, crampons and climbing gear.

The end result is papers, professional reports and PhD dissertations from up to 100 students each year. I told my passengers how they'd come into town each year to march in the Fourth of July parade, but in fact I had little idea at the time of what their life atop the icefield was all about.

Late in July of 1984, Dr. Miller told the local newspaper, the *Juneau Empire*, his research had convinced him a warming trend had started about 15 years earlier and was still under way. He and his students were finding abnormalities in weather trends since the 1960s, indicating significant warming due to strong build-up of carbon dioxide and other trace gases from burning of fossil fuels.

Most of us read the article as a passing curiosity. We hadn't tuned in to the now familiar concept of global warming. Nor did we realize that his assessment in 1984 was a sea change from what he'd thought 18 years earlier.

In 1966, as Dr. Miller was writing an article for *National Geographic* magazine's February 1967 issue, he believed the Juneau Icefield was telling a different story. He wrote that he believed smog and changing carbon dioxide would prove only marginal in effecting climate future. Glaciers were still healthy, some were surging forward. He quoted an affiliate who believed glaciers waxed and waned in concert with sunspots. The Mendenhall was proclaimed a healthy, active, growing glacier that would likely stabilize, and then begin a significantly speeded up advance in the next century.

In 1985 the Mendenhall made a small surge forward.

"If you're a Mendenhall Valley homeowner, you might want to know that one side of the Mendenhall Glacier is starting to creep in your direction," began a local news story on July 9 of that year. The right side of the glacier had started to advance. Well, that would be me, and I had a new line for my daily commentary. "I might get a new home," I'd tell my passengers.

I knew people were curious about where I lived, though only once did someone ask if they could see my house. Sometimes I pointed out our street as we drove past, but I was guarded about my personal life.

The same article revealed some of the mystery of the disappearing waterfall. A few years earlier the glacier had grown far enough to dam the normal channel of Nugget Creek, forming a lake nearly 200 feet deep between the glacier and the

Photo taken from Mendenhall Glacier Visitor Center in mid-1980s, with Nugget Falls just to the right of glacier face.

Photo taken from Mendenhall Glacier Visitor Center in 2010 with huge gap between face of glacier and Nugget Falls.

nearby rock wall. Then in 1984, that lake flooded over the top of its cavern and hollowed out a new, larger channel beneath the glacier's face, seamlessly discharging part of its water into Mendenhall Lake.

The advance was short-lived. A 1987 black and white photo at the visitor center shows the base of Nugget Falls clearly visible; the face of the Mendenhall had stepped back behind it. As the 20th century yielded to the 21st, the face was retreating at an annual rate 10 times what it had in 1984, at 150 to 300 feet a year. Glacial pace, if you mean to imply slow, had become an oxymoron.

Summer of 2004 brought a record 12 days above 80 degrees, nearly double the previous record. Salmon streams dried or slowed to a trickle. Rain slickers were tossed aside. Rare lightening crackled over Thunder Mountain. Glaciers lifted their face to the sun and calved and melted without restraint. The face of the Mendenhall calved with unusual intensity all summer, retreating backward 650 feet. Some 50 feet of ice melted from the top at its terminus. And the Mendenhall River, fed by glacial melt, surged toward the sea.

The retreat shows no sign of abating. From mid-May to early June in 2007, one section of the face retreated 470 feet alone. Over the course of the summer portions retreated a total of 700 feet.

Today the waterfall is so far removed from the face of the glacier it's hard for first time visitors to visualize how much the face of the glacier has changed in just over 25 years. The terminus has moved from a half-mile from the edge of the parking lot to well over a mile. Where the face once hovered 100 to 300 feet above the surface of the lake, it now slants down to meet the water, in places seemingly just a few yards above the lake. Local artists who once filled canvasses with bold blue and gray abstractions of the serrated face the height of a 30-story building find it a less appealing subject now.

Scientists say that in another decade the glacier could pull out of the lake it now fills with silt-laden melt, and retreat with dry feet back up the valley. If so, I hope I'm here to see what would have been unthinkable just a few decades ago.

But it's not likely the lake will suddenly drain down the Mendenhall River leaving a dry lake bed behind. Deep basins of water near the current face are more than 300 feet deep, and even near the parking lot the lake is up to 45 feet deep.

The flat farmlands where I grew up were the by-product of the Wisconsin Ice Age 10,000 years ago, but I saw only the aftermath. When I first moved north from the Midwest I had only the faintest notion of how a glacier would look. Many of my passengers had already crossed Alberta's Athabasca Glacier in the Columbia Icefield by fat-wheeled bus before arriving in Juneau, and the Mendenhall was less a mystery.

I'd tell them the Mendenhall was a remnant of the Little Ice Age, then try to explain how a glacier forms and what it means for a glacier to retreat.

The headwaters of this river of ice receive 100 to 200 feet of snow a year. If my passengers had a driveway anywhere in the temperate zone, that was a measure they could identify with. "It snows year-round up there," I'd say. Valley glaciers form when winter snowfall piles deeper than it can melt the following summer. As the snow pack builds to 150 feet deep, the bottom layers turn to ice under the weight of snow on top.

"It's like making a snowball and squeezing the air out until you have an ice ball," I'd say, reaching back into my childhood winters. I hoped my unscientific explanation was clear enough without sounding too silly or simplistic.

When the weight of 200 feet of ice and snow bears down, the ice on the bottom yields to pressure, becomes pliant and starts flowing downhill with enough strength to carve steep, sheer valleys and fjords out of bedrock. You've got to give that kind of power its due.

"At the same time the ice is moving down from above, it's melting and breaking off at the face," I'd continue, gesturing the movement with my hands. "When it calves or melts at the face faster than it flows down, the face actually retreats."

Dr. Miller and some of the Forest Service naturalists compared the process to a bank account, with deposits on top and withdrawals at the bottom. When withdrawals exceed deposits, there's a net loss. I liked the metaphor, but it had already been used, and I thought I should come up with my own explanation.

I preferred cool rainy days when mountains were shadows of themselves, wrapped in a gossamer envelope of mist. They not only felt right to me, but they made it easier to visualize what makes the coastal rainforest work. "When it's raining down here," as it usually was, "it's probably snowing up there," I'd say. I'd tell people how lucky they were to be here on such a day, and that the deep blue glacier photos they'd admired in books and calendars were photographed on days just like this.

It was a good time to answer another common question, "What makes the ice blue?"

Like countless other tour guides, I'd assure them glacial ice wasn't blue at all, but the most beautiful clear crystal. The ice

---

12. Ice Fishing

The dense ice melts slowly, and in earlier days many fishermen, including me and my husband, filled ice chests at Mendenhall Lake to keep their catch fresh until it could be refrigerated. Jerry and I walked up to the lake and lassoed the ice that had calved off from the glacier. We stuck it in the cooler to preserve the fish we would have caught, that was usually salmon and halibut. It would keep it cold for a long time, longer than the commercial ice.

was formed under such great pressure that it didn't have air bubbles like ice cubes from their refrigerator. And that solid ice made it a very good reflector of light.

"The ice absorbs all colors of the spectrum except blue, which it transmits back toward the sky." And though it didn't seem logical, the ice looked bluer under an overcast sky than under a clear one.

I'd show them how they could identify ice that had broken or split overnight by the intense deep blue color. "After it's exposed to air for even a day the ice develops tiny cracks on its face and no longer reflects light as well. It starts to look washed out," I'd add.

They all wanted to see it calve, or break off at the face. I assured them it would happen when they turned their back or went to the restroom. For all my trips to the glacier I remember seeing it calve only once. It's not like a salt water glacier, I said, where tides and ocean waves continually assault and undercut the face, undermining its stability. Much of the calving actually occurs in winter, and the lake is fullest with bergs when the lake ice first melts around May, releasing the icebergs held fast to the face all winter.

"Don't you get tired of coming here every day?" someone often asked. I answered honestly.

"No, I never do. It's different every time you see it." I allowed that on days off, when no ships were in port, I usually rode a bicycle from my house to the glacier to just enjoy it on my own.

On a good day, if ships were in port, Blue and I would each make two trips to the glacier, one in mid-morning and one in the afternoon.

One day Blue was sidelined because her van was in a repair shop. She offered to sell tours dockside to fill my van, while I just kept driving. I should have known I'd be busy—Blue's outgoing personality makes her a natural at selling.

Mid-morning, late morning, early afternoon, late afternoon—I drove four tours that day. Between the morning and afternoon tours, Blue lifted a bag through my van window. She'd picked up a hamburger and Coke at McDonald's to keep me going, but I'd have to wait until my passengers were inside the glacier visitor center before having time to eat. Blue still likes to remind me how she'd worked me until my "tail was dragging." What she never mentions, though, is her generous spirit. She would not accept any of the proceeds she'd helped me earn that day.

I frequently quoted John Muir. I own two copies of his seminal *Travels in Alaska*. One is a 1971 hardbound reprint of the original 1915 publication by Houghton Mifflin. The second, a paperback reissued by the Sierra Club for which he would become best known, bears liberal yellow highlighting of the quotes I lifted for my tour monologue.

Muir first steamed into Southeast Alaska in early summer, 1879, entitling the chapter of his first encounter "Alexander Archipelago and the Home I Found in Alaska." I could identify right away. That was how I felt when I first moved to this state. I liked his evangelical exuberance for nature and Alaska, his "glacier gospel," as he called it. He wrote in a florid language we're embarrassed to use today. It was safer to quote somebody else. At the Mendenhall Glacier I often recited words he wrote

---

13. First Ice

One of my passengers included a little boy from Mexico who was seeing ice for the first time. He wanted to take a chunk home. When I told him it would melt and turn to water, he started to cry. I found a small piece of ice near lake's edge and put it in a plastic bag. At the end of the tour I showed him how it melted and he smiled.

upon visiting Glacier Bay: ". . . and here, too, one learns that the world, though made, is yet being made; that this is still the morning of creation." I appreciated the fact that he spent his teens in my home state–I count him one of Wisconsin's greatest natural resources, along with visionary architect Frank Lloyd Wright, master painter Georgia O'Keeffe, and Aldo Leopold, a naturalist before anyone even used the word. (Leopold's classic *A Sand County Almanac* was first published in 1949, a year after he died while fighting a grass fire on a neighbor's farm.) All had piercing night vision, seeing with clarity into the dark unknown future still shrouded in mystery for the rest of us.

Muir went to the same university I did, exactly 100 years earlier. At Camp Randall, where I walked to Badger football games through crisp autumn leaves on blue sky days, he saw young men returning from the wreckage of the American Civil War.

And I liked the idea that John Muir was a tour guide too, and that people had been coming to see this place for a very long time.

On his first trip to Alaska Muir joined a charter aboard the river steamer *Cassiar* out of Wrangell, headed for what is now Haines. Cruising northward, his fellow passengers pressed him with familiar questions.

"Is that a glacier down in that cañon (canyon)? And is it all solid ice?"

"How deep is it?"

"You say it flows. How can ice flow?"

"And where does it come from?"

Muir answered, "From snow that is heaped up every winter on the mountains."

"And how, then, is the snow changed into ice?"

These were all questions I answered, though not nearly so well nor from the depth of his personal understanding.

Muir called the Mendenhall "Auk Glacier" for the Tlingit Auk Kwaan Indians living in this area, and early gold miners followed his lead. How many times have we Anglicized the music of Native names? Our glacier became the namesake of Thomas Corwin Mendenhall in 1892 while he was superintendent of the U.S. Coast and Geodetic Survey.

When the United States purchased Russian America in 1867, the border with Canada in what is now Southeast Alaska was largely unknown, unsurveyed and uncertain. An 1825 treaty between Russia and Great Britain described the boundary as following a range of mountains in Southeast parallel to the Pacific Coast, but in some places such mountains did not actually exist. No one cared much, I told my passengers, until the 1890s gold rush. Then Canada focused on a direct route to the Klondike gold fields by sea, setting their sights on Skagway and the now-deserted town of Dyea. The United States claimed an unbroken land link joining Southeast with the rest of the Alaska Territory.

In 1892 the United States and Canada agreed to a joint survey team, but it only concluded there was no clear boundary. Mendenhall was later named to the Alaska Boundary Commission responsible for surveying the international boundary between Canada and Alaska

By 1903 President Theodore Roosevelt gathered a committee of three Americans, two Canadians, and England's chief justice who sided with the Americans and rejected Canada's claim to a seaport. Surveying started in 1904 by boat, packhorse and backpack in the remote mountains. It wasn't until 1908 that the boundary was officially marked by a treaty.

By then Mendenhall had made an imprint considerably beyond lending his name to a glacier, both here and abroad. Though he never attended college himself he served as a U.S. university professor and president. He helped develop the Japanese government's meteorological system as a visiting professor at Tokyo Imperial University. While superintendent of U.S. Weights and Measures, he decided the fundamental standards of length and mass in the United States would be the international meter and kilogram, a decision that was later known as the Mendenhall Order. And he published one of the first attempts at stylometry, studying patterns in writing to verify authorship.

All that was more than I judged my passengers on vacation wanted to hear. I told them about the indeterminate border that suddenly mattered when gold was discovered, and about the bureaucrat in the right place at the right time. "We liked his name so much we not only named a glacier for him, we used it for the valley, the river, a peninsula, a car dealership and a mall."

The Mendenhall Glacier is not the only force at work in the Mendenhall Valley. There is another, so powerful it re-shaped vast areas of the north and opened them to development.

Steep Creek starts as a waterfall at 2,000-foot elevation on Thunder Mountain, but it's easily visible from the base. It hurls itself down without pause until it reaches the valley floor, crosses under the road and empties into Mendenhall Lake like a crystal arrow piercing milky silt-laden waters of the lake. Salmon somehow pushed through the silt of Mendenhall River and lake to the fresh water of Steep Creek to spawn.

I would point out the creek, top to bottom, as we stood near its banks. Lower Steep Creek was once shaded and bordered by willow and alder, a favorite photo stop for visitors bent on scenic photography. The narrow stream with rocks in the middle, shrubs on each side and mountains in the background was worthy of any calendar. Back when slides were the medium of choice for serious photographers, I filled several sheets of slide holders with its picturesque views.

Beavers moved into the valley with a vengeance by the mid-1990s, denuding banks and flooding trails and generally taking it upon themselves to change some of the views I liked best, including Lower Steep Creek.

With the alder, willow and cottonwood taking hold in the wake of the retreating glacier, beaver were quick to recognize their life couldn't get much better. Abundant ponds and slow streams were ideal sites for lodges; the luxuriant emerging growth provided easy food and ready building materials. Trapping had been closed for two decades and natural predators like wolves and brown bear were scarce.

Before 1990 beavers that immigrated into the area were promptly trapped live and moved before they could establish an active colony and begin plugging nearby culverts. They would be replaced by new immigrants within two or three years.

After 1990 the Forest Service started live trapping beaver in spring, but they overlapped elementary school field trips to the area. When a student on a school field trip triggered a live trap and needed help to get free, the issue of moving the beavers opened public debate. Beaver watching, or rather seeing evidence of their presence, was after all a neat part of a school trip. Beavers are usually only active during the early morning and evening hours. Because of the public interest, and because control was no longer needed for fisheries enhancement, the Forest Service decided to let the beavers stay and do what they do best. Within 10 years they had occupied 17 of the area's 20 largest ponds, constructed 14 lodges and flooded 20 acres.

There are no homes or commercial property near the glacier imperiled by their insistence on creating wetlands, but beaver did threaten to disrupt one of the most popular attractions in mid-summer: salmon spawning. Wire beaver baffles were wedged into some dams to assure salmon could make it upstream where visitors could see them, until a new Steep Creek Salmon Viewing Trail was designed. Steep Creek beavers that threatened to damage a road bed were removed, but beavers in Lower Steep Creek were left alone because dams there actually improved habitat for coho salmon.

I recall seeing a beaver only twice while at the glacier with tourists, which is not surprising since the beavers are mainly nocturnal and are designed to swim and work under water, with little use for land except to harvest trees for dam building. Most of their tree-cutting is done at night.

The semi-aquatic rodent is covered with a heavy chestnut brown coat over silky gray underfur. That was its misfortune. The fur was highly prized in the European market after their numbers were decimated there. Nearly three million beaver pelts were sold to England between 1853 and 1877.

In the early 1800s beaver pelts were a medium of exchange between the Hudson Bay Company and Tlingit Indians who inhabited Southeast Alaska. The Tlingit traded beaver, fox, lynx, marten, mink, muskrat, otter and sea otter for awls, axes, blankets, buttons, beads, cloth, knives, scissors and rifles. The worth of each item was equated in beaver skins. Ten muskrat or four mink equaled one beaver. A prime sea otter was worth 12 beaver.

Hudson Bay also paid Native American trappers for beaver pelts with wool blankets, called Hudson's Bay point blankets. The blankets were graded by weight and size using a point system; higher points meant the blanket would be larger and warmer. The now-familiar classic pattern featured green, red, yellow and indigo stripes on a white background.

The beaver was so important in opening Canada through fur trade that it was named the national animal of Canada, portrayed on their five-cent piece and on their first postage stamp, the Three Penny Beaver. Its engineering skills made it the mascot for Massachusetts Institute of Technology, California Institute of Technology, Oregon State University and the University of Toronto, a fitting choice as only humans have changed the landscape more.

I liked to go out by the glacier early in the morning before other people were around, when songs of birds and falling water were the only sounds. One morning I led a couple who were spending a few days in Juneau to my beloved Lower Steep Creek, before it was deforested and while it still remained one of my favorite photo spots.

When we arrived, a bright orange salmon fillet draped over a rock mid-stream grabbed our immediate attention. My passengers grasped pretty quickly how the fish came to be there and were noticeably uncomfortable. I always carried a canister of Counter Assault® (capsaicin pepper spray), developed by bear biologists, in case of a close-up encounter with a bear. I routinely pointed it out to passengers and showed them how it was hooked over the waistband of my pants in a black Velcro holster. Sometimes it seemed to reassure them, sometimes it made them more nervous. Thankfully, I never had to retrieve it from amid the binoculars, tripod and spotting scope I also carried.

---

14. A Bear a Day

I had almost daily encounters with bears while living in a cabin at Lemon Creek. One morning while leaving for work, I saw one jump out of our boat parked next to the cabin. Another time, while stopping in to get lunch, I saw movement through the glass-window at the door. I chased that bear off the porch by turning on the TV full blast. The bear took off, stomping through my tomato plants.

The following year she returned, stopping off proudly with her cub as if to say, "See what I got." They were on their way to the city dump, where there was always a guarantee of food. On rainy days it was a great stop for eagle photography as well.

The few black bear we'd spotted had been from the security of the van. Only once did I become nervous myself. I was alone with two women on a forest trail on North Douglas Island (a group of four was the minimum size I considered large enough to dissuade advances from passing bear). We were headed back toward the van, perhaps just 150 feet away, at the end of our walk. I didn't hear anything out of the ordinary, didn't see anything. Suddenly I was assailed by the most offensive odor, unlike anything I'd ever smelled. I didn't know what a bear smelled like and I still don't. But with their legendary reputation for halitosis, I've always believed a bear was uncomfortably nearby. When I took visitors to the glacier in May I'd set up my tripod and spotting scope on the parking lot sidewalk. It's an ideal time to see mountain goats when they're low on mountainsides throughout Southeast Alaska. In summer they move to high alpine meadows, feeding on grasses and low shrubs. Even though their white fur stands out against the rocks it usually took me a while to find them.

"If it's white and it moves, it's a mountain goat," I'd say, enlisting my passengers' help in scanning the side of Mt. Bullard with binoculars before focusing with the scope.

"Hold your hand over the other eye and try not to touch the scope," I'd say after locating goats in the spotting scope lens. I extended it to the full 60-power magnification, and at that strength the smallest vibration would make the image inside too fuzzy. A 10-power is about the strongest binocular you can hand-hold and still see clearly.

By the early 1980s hunters wiped mountain goats from their Mt. Juneau habitat directly above downtown. Hunting season was closed in 1982. People who missed seeing goats joined with Alaska Department of Fish & Game, local businesses and Juneau Audubon Society to restore them to their former range. In August 1989, three billies and eight nannies were captured in Tracy Arm 50 miles south, lifted by helicopter and released at the base of Mt. Juneau near the road leading into the basin between Mt. Juneau and Mt. Roberts. True to their nature, they climbed the mountain and spread out through the area.

Now they're once again thriving, visible from downtown offices, cruise ship docks and the top of the Mt. Roberts tram.

The regular habitat of mountain goats is so remote and inaccessible that when Captain Cook got goat hides in the late 1700s he assumed they were white bear. Later they were mistaken for Dall sheep, though goats are easily distinguished from sheep by their longer cream-colored coat, deep chest and shorter black horns. They live out most of their lives at or above tree line to avoid predators like wolves and bears. Large hoofs allow them to climb rocky cliffs at a 60-degree slope or more, wintering as high as 9,000 feet at minus 50 degrees F., in winds up to 100 miles per hour. Only in spring, when females go off alone to give birth at low elevations, are they so accessible, and so vulnerable.

Travelers in May 2006 were witness to just how vulnerable.

The glacier visitor center has its own spotting scopes for visitors, and Forest Service rangers had been using them to show off a mountain goat kid all afternoon. Kids, usually just one, are born in late May or early June. They're so precocious they can keep up with adults only hours after birth. This one had been sighted just a week earlier. Onlookers were enchanted by the protective nanny and her offspring.

Over the course of the afternoon a staff member noticed a black bear and her cub on the same slope, meandering ever closer to the goats. Suddenly the sow bolted straight up the knoll toward the herd of goats with startling speed. The nanny positioned herself between the bear and her kid; two other female goats ran at the bear. But they were no match. The bear charged through the guard, grabbed the hapless kid, dragged it into nearby bushes and proceeded to tear it apart and eat it while the goats stood helplessly by.

Visitors were dazed. Forest Service staff who routinely see bear and other wildlife around them, were equally astounded and shocked at the raw *National Geographic* moment.

The nature of things is not always pretty but it is always changing, always full of surprises.

"What does the glacier look like in winter?" people often asked us, wondering perhaps if it simply disappeared. My most memorable winter image to date occurred a few years after the last visitor had exited my van.

In late November our days are not merely short, they simply fail to show up. Gray flannel skies have not yet made the transition from dropping rain to sloughing snow. What little light there is will be absorbed by the black asphalt roadways and thick dark stands of spruce and hemlock. Mountains that begin their steep climb from sea level just blocks away obliterate huge hunks of sky.

You need to know the area and play close attention to find actual light of day, to calculate where the sun will find a clear path to the earth as it travels low through the northern sky. Thus it was an unexpected gift when shards of November sunlight illuminated the snow-capped Chilkat Mountains and glanced on the sinewy curves of flowing ice atop the Mendenhall Glacier. Threading through quiet streets of my neighborhood, I came to the traffic signal and stopped for a red light. My destination was our local Super Bear grocery store and their deli fried chicken, a left turn and a mile away. But my white minivan instinctively turned right and headed for the glacier. Tourists were long gone, of course, and I wondered if mine would be the only vehicle as I approached the visitor center parking lot.

What was I thinking? The glacier is never alone. Locals are under its spell as much as visitors are. Its power to draw people to itself in any weather, in every season, is inexplicable and undeniable. In every month, in any weather, it draws us in.

Even with more trips here than I could count, I was not prepared for the November view that awaited me. A brilliant, wide rainbow ran floor to ceiling on Mt. McGinnis to the left. The glacier itself was a sculpture of light and shadow, with deep blue spots revealing cracking ice newly exposed to the air. If you could melt into such a scene and become one with it, your spirit could soar without limits.

I could not take my eyes away. If I could have a last vision before dying, I thought, I would choose this moment. I looked around hungrily, trying to absorb it all, led Tucker, my little black dachshund, on a leash and looked around again. At last remembering that I went out to pick up chicken for lunch, I reluctantly returned to the van. But I wanted to make one more stop before the grocery store. Driving toward the glacier, I noticed an inordinate number of ravens and magpies gathered in a small pull-off by a lake that hosts summer sockeye salmon runs. There is a late fall salmon run as well, and I supposed one of the birds had dropped a fish on the pavement. Something was attracting them. I was pretty sure they hadn't gathered for the scenery that so entranced me.

I left the glacier view parking lot and pulled into the lakeside parking area the equivalent of a block away. Lying a few yards from the van on the blacktop was the leg of a deer, still hoofed and covered in fur. Just inside a thick stand of spruce, perhaps 20 feet from my van, a black bear looked up from feeding. A few feet away, another bear fed. To be so close they must have been mother and offspring, I thought, though they were nearly the same size.

Our eyes met, as naturally as I might look into Tucker's eyes, from the protective bubble of my minivan. Eye contact is not recommended for a chance encounter on a trail, when it might be perceived by the bear as a threat. Here I was free from the instinctive quickening of heartbeat and breathing; there was no such danger.

But even now I did not linger. Tucker was lying on the seat and hadn't yet seen the bears through the window I'd hastily closed. I didn't want his barking to agitate the bears and create a threat to someone passing by unaware on foot or bicycle.

I pulled away regretfully, stopped up the road to warn a woman walking a dog, and drove to Super Bear for chicken.

6. Why We Travel

"What are you looking at?"

Among my first purchases for my fledgling business were a Bausch and Lomb zoom spotting scope and a tripod for close-up looks at anything of interest to me, and by my reasoning, of interest to everyone else. Early in the season, May and June, I'd carry them over a paved path to a rocky promontory in front of the glacier, the scope hung over my left arm and the tripod resting on my right shoulder like a rifle. After extracting the lens from its carrying case I'd screw it onto the tripod base to steady it, point it toward the ground, adjust the focus, zoom it in to the full 60x magnification, then stand back in pride as though I could take credit for what was encapsulated in the lens.

My passengers' attention would be directed to the base of a Nootka lupine, a stalk of blue flowers visitors had already likened to the Texas Blue Bonnet. Arctic Tern nested there, in a dimple in the sand left by the retreating glacier.

"If seagulls with their fat bodies were 747's, Arctic Terns would be Concordes," I'd say. That was the era when Concordes were still flying with that sleek trim body and downward pointed nose that reminded me of a tern hovering in flight, diving for fish. With their penchant for ceaseless travel, black caps, deep forked tail and bright red bill and legs, Arctic Terns are designer birds in every sense. How could my passengers not admire them?

I was raising the curtain on a small miracle, but most people, lured north by showier creatures, didn't seem much interested.

I persisted. "They're Arctic Terns," I said. "They've come here from the tip of South America to nest. They have the longest known migratory path in the world. These terns have traveled 11,000 miles one way."

It is birds who are the ultimate travelers. Their flights are so instinctual that some young of the year depart for wintering grounds even before their parents leave to lead the way. How else would they know where and when to go?

For us, travel is as old as our nagging curiosity about what's in the next village, around the bend. Tourism is as old as our tentative nature about leaving the comfortable familiarity of home, the sense that we want help in finding our way in an unfamiliar world.

The real adventurers slip into local culture, seek out what is different and embrace the dangers, physical or political.

---

15. Building Bonds

At the beginning of my tour, I asked everyone where they were from so they could get acquainted. Several times people lived close together—almost neighbors, as close as 12 miles apart—and they didn't know each other until they met in my van.

When I had passengers from the state of Oregon, I mentioned the name of a dear friend of my husband and me, Bob Blaine, who is author of *North to Alaska*. And they also knew him!

Human bonds were established while traveling in small groups in our vans.

For most of us, our biggest baggage is our comfort zone and we are loathe to leave it behind. We all take at least two journeys, one to satisfy need or curiosity, the other to navigate the daunting maze inside. In the end, our greatest journey is the journey within. The best trips allow us to plumb those depths as well as the call of distant lands.

In *The Art of Travel*, Alain de Botton wrote there is "danger that we may see things at the wrong time, when we are not receptive to them."

"Why do you travel?"

"Because there's only so many Christmas trees you're going to buy," says Peter, a friend with a failing kidney.

"To get away from your daily routine and see something new," said my sister-in-law Helena, who lives in a north woods lakeside home worthy as a vacation getaway in its own right.

"It just gets in motion," says Kathy, another friend whose destinations have included Mongolia, China, India, Belgium, Ireland. Her domestic destinations are normally limited to family and to high school friendships which have remained intact for decades.

"I'm forever working on a travel philosophy, because I want one. I want to know where I want to go and what I want to do and how long I want to stay and under what circumstances. I don't want to wake up some day and wish I had done something," she says.

In 1899 a physician prescribed a long vacation for his exhausted patient, Edward Henry Harriman. The railroad magnate chose Alaska for a family holiday and bear hunt. Then he asked C. Hart Merriman, one of the country's most prominent scientists, to help choose other scientists, authors and artists to accompany him for an all-expenses-paid two-month scientific expedition to the Alaskan coast. The group included John Burroughs, best-selling nature writer of the day; John Muir, father of the American conservation movement;

photographer Edward Curtis; and George Bird Grinnell, editor of *Field & Stream*, founder of the Audubon Society, advisor to Theodore Roosevelt and prime mover in creation of Glacier National Park.

With 126 passengers and crew it was the largest and most famous expedition the world had yet seen, and the story of their May 31 departure from Seattle aboard the *George W. Elder* appeared on the front pages of newspapers from around the world.

As on today's cruises, life was anything but rustic on board. Guests enjoyed newly-refurbished cabins and salons, and gourmet meals. They could browse a library of over 500 books about Alaska and on many days could listen to a scientist lecturing about his area of expertise. An organ, piano, tents, hunting gear and art supplies were all loaded aboard.

---

16. Silver Spoons

If she could have only seen this, he said, as tears trickled down his weather-beaten face. His hands shook as he faced the Mendenhall Glacier. He said his wife had passed away seven years ago.

"Would you drop me off in town after the tour? I'm looking for two silver spoons that I want to buy for my daughters." Of course I would.

While admiring one of God's creations, he was thinking of his loved ones. Paps came from a long line of Dutch immigrants who had settled this country in the 1600s. They were diamond cutters. His father was an iron molder. He described some of the iron molds that he still had in his home.

It made him so happy to be able to talk to someone to share a sliver of his life. I took the group, including Paps, back to town and showed him where he could buy the silver spoons. He left my tour a happy man.

Shore time was too brief for in-depth exploration, just as today, but scientists and naturalists made careful observations while the Harriman family hunted grizzly and vacationed. After traveling as far as Plover Bay, Siberia, and St. Lawrence Island, the *Elder* headed back south and steamed into Seattle on July 30. They returned with more than 100 trunks of specimens and more than 5,000 photographs and colored illustrations.

A century and one-half earlier, in 1741, Georg Wilhelm Steller sailed here with Vitus Bering and barely touched land, but he described the North American turquoise and black jay that now bears his name. The Steller's sea cow, also named for him, was hunted to extinction less than three decades later.

Perhaps it's not the length of our travels, but our focus, that gives them legs. With logistics so much easier today, it's likewise easier to travel with no purpose save escaping the daily routine—traveling to get away as much as to get to.

"Why do you travel?" Blue and I asked a rugged-faced woman gazing at the glacier.

"To convince myself that home is still best," she said. The corner she claimed as her home, Point Reyes north of San Francisco.

It's easy to forget that the places we travel are someone else's home; not everyone is a tourist like we are.

When I was no longer leading tours I'd walk Tucker near the glacier parking lot, a destination I routinely picked not only because it offered easy walks for him but because I needed a regular glacier fix myself. One morning as we threaded our way among early season cruise ship travelers, one woman looked at us and asked "How did he get here?" She seemed genuinely taken aback when I said "He lives here."

My passengers might have been surprised to know that I was as curious about them as they were about Alaska. Sometimes I'd mentally spin stories to imagine details I had no way of knowing.

One overcast July morning a man I judged in his 40s climbed into my van wearing a bandage around his forehead. "I had brain surgery five weeks ago," he said matter-of-factly, but with a note of pride and defiance. A young teen-age boy was traveling with him, about 14, slim build, with features that were even and pleasant but undistinguished. "His son," I thought. The boy was quiet, maybe a bit uncomfortable. I sensed they didn't know each other as well as a father and son ought.

His parents didn't live together, I guessed. They lived in different states, perhaps, or cross-continent. The father had likely arranged this vacation with his son months ago. Maybe he had even gone to court over the right to take his son so far from his mother's home. Alaska still seemed more like a foreign country than one of the 50 states back then. No mere brain surgery would rob him of this precious time with his son.

For two years Eaglecrest, the local city-owned ski resort on Douglas Island, experimented with running a lift for summer sightseeing. The lift seats were big plastic eggs, with a thin bar that latched across the front to hold riders in place two abreast while their legs dangled below. On the few days without rain those two summers, views from the top were spectacular. The rewards for a short hike from the top of the lift to the ridge were alpine slopes adorned with wildflowers, mountaintop vistas of islands and sea, and a heady sense of being above the clouds. I gave little thought to the lift itself.

Then one day I found myself seated next to a young woman who was traveling solo. She'd signed up for my sightseeing and ski lift combo and I was her travel companion for the afternoon. We were halfway up the mountain, the ground falling ever further below us, when she turned to me and said, "I wanted to take this tour because I'm afraid of heights."

I froze. Would I soon be dealing with a panic attack?

"You've got to be the grown-up," I told myself. When people were nervous about boarding small aircraft or helicopters I'd wear a bright smile and exude reassurance and matter-of-factness. "I'd never book someone on a tour I wouldn't do myself," I'd tell them.

Now I felt my fanny sliding forward on the smooth seat. I realized for the first time how easy it would be to slip beneath the bar to the mountainside below. Wriggling backward as far as I could, I stole a discreet look at traveler beside me. She had a peaceful smile as though she had at that moment overcome her fear. I put on my reassuring smile and tried not to think about how I felt vulnerable on these lifts for the first time. We made the trip up and down the mountain easily, without incident, but the lift never looked the same to me after that day.

Many people I met were afraid of flying, but they had few options in this far-flung area of few roads and great distances. One was married to a man who came to Alaska to pursue his dream of photographing every mammal in North America. He weighed twice as much as many adults, and they were traveling

---

17. Revisiting a Moving Landmark

I stood at the ramp, watching the docking of the *Island Princess* while holding my sign. An elderly man walked up to me and said, "Would you please take me to the Mendenhall Glacier? I had seen the glacier last in 1938." I told him, "You are in for a surprise. Maybe you should give the glacier tour."

When I told him that we now had a new highway, he showed me a picture of a cow path which at that time led to the glacier. In the horse and buggy days, people of Juneau had taken the ice from the glacier, transported it into town, and sold it in bars and grocery stores.

He showed me the spot where the face of the glacier had been, as he remembered it, in 1938. He could hardly fathom the change.

in a four-place commuter plane for 90 miles. She confessed to me later how frightened she had been, and I admired her refusal to give in to fear.

Another woman found herself boarding a commuter plane after weather delayed reservations on jet and ferry. She was nervous until she learned the pilot, a woman, had the same first name as her sister. "That was my message it would be all right," she said.

"Why do people travel?" I asked the owner of successful gift shops in two ports of call, Juneau and Skagway. To escape pressures at work, he ventured. On a cruise "butchers and firemen can feel rich for a short time. They want no-hassle, unpack-once vacations."

Blue and I collaborated on our most creative and ambitious tour, designed for a class of 14 seventh grade gifted students from the Midwest. It was led by their teacher and his wife, and included their two school-aged daughters. We chartered helicopter flights to Maynard Miller's research station atop the Juneau Ice Cap, scheduled a briefing with a Native-owned corporation created by the 1971 Alaska Native Claims Settlement Act, arranged a beach walk with a local naturalist who harvested and stir-fried beach greens for lunch, and led them on a trail overlooking the Mendenhall Glacier.

The young teens went charter fishing for salmon; got a private tour of the Victorian House of Wickersham, once home to Judge James Wickersham, a pioneer judge, statesman, delegate to Congress, author and historian who imprinted nearly every facet of Alaska's heritage in the first 39 years of the last century. They cruised Tracy Arm glacier fjord, toured the Alaska State Museum and ate spaghetti on my back deck.

While I was caught up, and frankly feeling a bit smug, about the experiences Blue and I had conjured up and brought into being, there was another agenda at play between the leaders. The couple had met in Alaska, married and moved back to their home state. It gradually became clear he hoped this trip would spark his family's interest in a return to living in Alaska. It was not to be—neither wife nor daughters shared his dream. They reminded me of how often this land divides couples, when one does not share the other's passion for living here.

I wonder if any of the young people in that group have returned north, or taken a path in their life as a result of their travels here. I wish I'd taken time from focusing on the logistics of making this tour happen to get to know just a bit more about them.

Many travelers we met were genuinely interested in their destination, and read well beyond the tourist hype brochures before and during their trip. One woman brought a 900-page paperback version of James A. Michener's novel, *Alaska*. She

18. White Elbows

It was foggy when we landed at the edge of a cliff on the Juneau Ice Cap. Precaution had to be taken to get everyone off safely. Do not ever go behind the helicopter. If they had, they would have sailed several thousand feet down to the valley. Food and people were flown in, garbage out.

The helicopters returned to the heliport at sea level as students were briefed on the ongoing research by Dr. Miller and his staff inside one of the field stations.

I had to use an outhouse at the edge of a cliff which was freshly painted on the inside. Space was very narrow. When I tried to pull up my pants, I got stuck with both elbows on each side of the walls. My brand-new Columbia jacket now sported white elbows and I wore it proudly during the rest of the season. Made a great story when someone asked. After the fog lifted, I was able to video students' experiences on top of the mountain.

ripped out and read sections pertinent to where she and her husband were traveling at the time, discarding them when she was through to make reading the entire tome seem less formidable.

One traveler said he had come here to retrace the route of his brother who had worked over the border in Canada. His brother had been about to board a helicopter when a young mother and child headed into the path of the spinning rotor. He moved quickly to shove them from harm's way, and lost his own life instead. "That was so like him," said the man who was inhaling the north as though he was breathing in the essence of his brother's spirit.

One rainy afternoon—weren't they all?—a family grouping came into my van. All together they numbered five or six, but I only remember one. A slight woman in her late 30's or early 40's, she had short dark hair and a contorted face. She was no longer able to walk, and two men formed a human chair by

---

19. Travel Has Many Faces

On a flight from Denver to Seattle in 2008 the lady next to me had buried her face in her arms, thrown a coat over herself and slept. The flight attendant and I could not waken her for breakfast. Must have been a rough night, I thought. When she finally awoke, we started talking. She was a metal inspector working in the Prudhoe Bay oil field on Alaska's North Slope. She was just returning from two-week R&R in Denver and had to fly to Anchorage, then Prudhoe Bay where she would arrive at 8 p.m. and sleep in the camp so she could return to work the next day. My travel companion, her name was Mercedes, had worked in 50 below zero temperatures where people can only stay out for a few minutes at a time. Her co-worker had

locking arms beneath and around her. She winced with every move. I guessed she'd sooner be left alone in her pain, but she had a family who cared much for her and wanted to give her the trip of a lifetime before hers ended too soon

It's no surprise romance thrives on the high seas, away from the constraints and inhibitions imposed by office decorum, daily demands and personal acquaintances. A newspaper article purported to give the high percentage of couples who had sex within an hour of sailing. Shopping for tee-shirts wasn't the first thing on their minds.

One day a couple entered my van, so attractive I can picture them to this day. She wore a tight pink short-sleeved sweater perfectly molded to her shapely top. At the very tip of her pointy, perky left breast, she wore a small gold pin, most likely a frat pin. I hadn't seen that since my own college days, a little short of the sexual revolution. His blue plaid shirt was neatly tucked into belted brown slacks, with no hint of a paunch; his

gone out for six minutes—too long—and her glasses froze to her face. When she tried to take them off, skin came off along with the glasses.

Mercedes had left three children behind in Denver. In parting in Seattle we wished each other a good life.

Her travel was a necessity. But I had moved to Denver and mine was just about visiting dear friends in Alaska, going fishing with my stepson in Petersburg, and wandering through memory lane.

In the waiting room in Seattle, where I had disembarked to change planes, I sat next to a lady who was 86 years old. She was traveling to Juneau to visit her 14th great grandchild. She was so full of life even though she had had 16 operations, was missing one kneecap and hobbled with a cane. The flight attendant came with a wheel chair. I helped her into it and we bid goodbye before we boarded the flight for Juneau.

It had been cloudy in Seattle. Now we were flying over snow-covered mountains and glaciers of Southeast Alaska. One could only marvel at that landscape that I had fallen in love with so many years ago. The sun was shining—a beautiful day. My heart swelled. It was like coming home. Red was flying to New York for the summer just as I was arriving for my visit. At least there would be time for a hug at the airport between the time my plane landed and her plane boarded. We had about five minutes together. Then it was on to Petersburg for me. I had expected to board soon after.

But at 5:30 p.m., three and one-half hours after I had said goodbye to Red, I was still in Juneau waiting for my plane which was delayed by mechanical difficulties. I bought a halibut melt with fries and Coke—cost was $17 (those are Paris prices!). The frozen sausage in my carry-on bag was getting soft.

I had a great view of the Mendenhall Glacier through the airport restaurant windows, and watched helicopters flying by carrying cruise ship passengers on a tour to the glacier. Red had told me that six cruise ships were in town on this day and that one million visitors were expected through the summer.

Time passed, and there was no sign of the part for my plane to Petersburg. Every half hour another delay

---

brown hair was perfectly groomed. They could have been Barbie and Ken. I kept staring despite my best effort to look away. You could have encircled her waist with a medium-size dog collar and her slim hips were very, well, Barbie. Walking

was announced until 10 p.m., when we would be given a coupon for a stay at a nearby motel. Other than that, I was fine. Hell of a day. Why do people travel? To be punished?

It was still daylight. After checking in at the motel and depositing the thawing sausage in the motel freezer, I took a walk in drizzling rain. I bought a bear claw sweet roll and a bagel at the 24-hour Breeze Inn deli. At 3 a.m., I got up and tried to take a shower. No hot water; the coffee pot didn't operate either. I took the shuttle back to the airport. By now TSA had seen my baggage three times, but I had to take out my meds and that darned sausage again.

Now we were off to Ketchikan (I'd already flown over that town on my way to Juneau), to wait for a plane from Seattle that would take us to Petersburg. In Ketchikan I talked with another lady, who was from Wrangell. She mentioned a dear fried of hers, Doreen. I could not believe it, for the same Doreen was also a dear friend of mine while I lived in Juneau. She asked how Doreen was doing and I had to tell her the sad news that Doreen had passed on.

I had a yogurt and coffee mocha, and retrieved my bagel from the night before and spread it with mayonnaise. Yuk. My hips felt like they were locking from so much sitting. I called friends in Petersburg. They said that when I arrived, I would go straight to Kito's Kave for my stepdaughter's birthday party. But first I had to find a freezer for that darned sausage.

---

down the sidewalk near the glacier they shared a secret laugh and she playfully reached for his crotch. Were they on an anniversary cruise? Was it an illicit tryst? It was a giddy romance in a couple I judged to be in their 40's.

.

"Why do you travel?," I asked a longtime friend in Juneau. "To get from one place to another to see someone I want to see," answered the mother and grandmother of family living in Oklahoma and Oregon. She has since moved to Paris, and now her children and grandchildren travel to France to visit her there.

A retired college professor and inveterate traveler had just returned from a bus tour to Alaska when I asked him why he travels. "I like to know things. I like to see things. I like to test myself," he said. "I like to push myself and get into tough places." He normally plans his own itineraries, he said, but "if you're going to a place you don't know, a tour is a good way to go." Overall it was quite a good tour, he said. "The kitschy crap was minimal and not too intrusive." "Did anything surprise you?" I asked. He said he is a knowledgeable traveler and is seldom surprised.

When his Alaskan bus tour guide learned he was an English professor, she asked him to read the Robert Service poem, "The Creation of Sam McGee," aloud. He knew most of it by heart at the age of 15, he told me, and when he finished his recitation, the guide said, "It doesn't get any better than that." At the tour's farewell dinner party, the guide presented him with a coffee mug with a moose head in relief on one side and text on the other that reads "May your cup always be two turds full." In the bottom are two ceramic moose turds. "I love it. I use it all the time," he said.

I laughed. "None of us is above kitsch," I said.

7. It Smells Fishy

Most of the people who entered my van from a cruise ship remain as only fragments in my memory, bits and pieces of who they were and why they traveled north. A few stand out still.

"Take good care of my precious cargo."

Her smile was broad, her voice chipper. But the pleading was unmistakable when her eyes locked into mine. She was a tour guide and escort for some 30 people aboard a cruise ship at the dock, assigned to keep them safe and happy around the clock. It's a job much harder than it might appear.

I was an unknown on the streets of a city far from the places any of them called home, and she was entrusting 10 of her charges to a road trip with me. Her eyes told me she hoped it would not be a mistake.

They climbed into my van, a contented group she had clearly served well. Most were couples. When I had solo travelers in a group I often invited them to sit in the front seat beside me. The couples seemed happy to sit together on the benches and for the singles it seemed a good reprieve from the sometimes awkwardness of traveling without a companion.

On this day the single was a woman I guessed to be in her 50's, with brown hair and a large open face. She wore dark slacks, a beige mid-calf duster with a tie belt and the trianglar head scarf favored in the 1950s. A pleasant front-seat companion, she asked about the weather and what it was like to live here in winter—standard stuff. She didn't talk to distraction, a quality I always counted a plus.

When we returned to the dock two and one-half hours later, their escort was waiting for us.

"We're back," I said brightly. All my passengers seemed happy. She was visibly relieved.

I'm not sure when I first noticed it, the smell wafting from the van's front seat. It was probably early afternoon, as I was preparing for my second tour of the day. The seats were covered in beige fabric upholstery, not the leather or vinyl more forgiving of daily use. Fabric came with its warmth and its vulnerability.

I sprayed air freshener directly onto the front passenger seat, which had an odor I couldn't identify. I do remember seeing the solo woman disembark that morning with no tell-tale stains on her light-colored coat. That I would have noticed. The seat upholstery was not wet, not even damp. There were no visible stains. Nothing seemed amiss. Nothing but the smell.

My mind raced over the possibilities. I thought back to a Sammy Cohen concert in San Francisco. Cohan had leaned, sophisticated and urbane, against an ebony grand piano, compelling even on the exit side of middle age. Throughout the evening a parade of gorgeous young women in elegant evening gowns stood next to him and gave seemingly effortless voice to his songs. It was heady stuff for a tourist from a northern outpost. But just as memorable was the woman in a front row seat.

She entered after we did, her blond hair teased and fluffed. She wore a black wool skirt, gold wool jacket, gold charm bracelet and other gold jewelry that was clearly real and expensive. A trophy wife, I'd sniff today. She was giggly, giddy, and very, very drunk. When she stood up at intermission and the upholstered seat cushion sprang up behind her, liquid dripped from the cushion to the floor. I hadn't noticed her carrying a cocktail glass into the theater, and we laughed that she must have peed onto the seat. Her black skirt was unmarked, which convinced me you could wear black and nothing would ever ever show.

Is this what happened sometime during my tour, I wondered, and I hadn't realized it?

The next morning I opened the driver's door for my nine-mile trip from home to the dock and the smell was still there, only worse, like wet socks aged at the bottom of the hamper. I bypassed air fresheners with names like Mountain Mist and Fresh Rain and reached for Lysol, hoping that somehow my passengers would not notice.

For a week the odor permeated my van. I sprayed air freshener on the seat and in the air several times a day. I opened windows and doors between tours, all to no avail. Everyone was too polite to mention it, perhaps thinking I was the source. How could that woman have peed and not marked a beige polished cotton coat? And it didn't smell like that. It was stronger. More acrid. More menacing. It began to haunt me. It was the smell of death, I thought, the smell of decaying, putrefying flesh. Had someone sat there who was that ill, and I did not recognize it? Had I looked right through her without seeing her pain? Was this her last great trip on this earth, and had she spent part of it with me?

Or was she cursed with this odor every day?

The memory lingered in my mind years after the odor finally faded. Finally, I had to look for a probable cause. Via the internet I learned about a disorder called trimethylaminuria, more common in women, only recently understood and still unfamiliar to many health professionals though it has been around for centuries. Victims are often too embarrassed to seek help and when they do poor hygiene may be blamed. Its nickname pretty well sums it up: the fish odor syndrome. Trimethylamine accumulates in bodies of people unable to break it down, finally escaping through breath and body fluids as it leaves victims smelling like rotting garbage. A cruel condition, it burdens social and professional relationships and causes depression. The odor can spread from the victim's office to the ventilation system and over an entire office floor.

There is no cure save prevention by avoiding foods with chorine like eggs, fish, peas, beans and organ meats like liver.

Would trimethylaminuria have been recognized and treated back in the mid-1980s? Did this woman and those around her live with it every day? If so, why couldn't I smell it on her in the van? Or was it really a symptom of a life-threatening illness, and did my front seat passenger know what lay ahead? I would never know. As with most of the people who entered my van in Juneau, she and I would share only a brief encounter.

Some snippets of memory just make me smile. My jewelry box holds a polished rock teardrop on a gold chain, in mottled shades of beige and gray with an onyx tip. It was a gift from a cruise ship traveler I drove to the glacier with his wife. He carried a plastic bag filled with stones he had polished in a workshop tumbler, and freely gave them to people he met.

"Pick whichever one you like," he said, holding the open bag toward me. I chose one in my favorite earth tones, imagining it with English tweeds I fancied myself wearing in those years when I needed a walking stick. Even yet I like to think of this man's stones scattered in familiar places and many I've never heard of.

Passengers Blue and I met and picked up downtown were typically couples traveling post-retirement. They were pursuing adventures long-postponed to raise and educate children, see them safely married and welcome grandchildren. But this trio sto od apart.

They were three generations of women—at least that's what they appeared to be. I can't recall they actually told me that. The middle one, in her 30's, wore a long, single blond braid reaching mid-way down her back, and a white peasant blouse with red and blue embroidery. The young girl—her daughter, I assumed—looked about 10. The elder, presumably the grandmother, would have been late 50's, early 60's. They all wore light clothes, in light colors, peasant styles popular two decades earlier. It must have been one of our uncharacteristically warm, dry days.

I don't remember how we connected; the women were overnighting rather than coming by cruise ship. I do remember it was a slow day, and the unlikely trio received a private tour of the city, the glacier, the chapel—three passengers in a van designed to hold 14. We covered all the sights as leisurely as though I had a full payload. Truth be told, I liked the small groups, which says right off I was no businesswoman. When I was in the eighth grade, I was asked in a sidewalk poll if I'd rather have a job I enjoyed or one that earned a lot of money. Without hesitation I picked the former, and nothing had changed in the intervening years.

The mid-1980s were still a relatively trusting time here, and we often collected the fare at the end of a tour rather than up-front. On this day I pulled up to the State Museum, our last stop, and the younger woman handed me a $100 bill. While I carried cash for change, on this particular morning I didn't have the right denominations. Ever anxious to dispel the notion that the local tour operators were less than honest, I left her $100 bill on the back of my seat while I went into the museum shop to change a twenty for two tens. And it was still there when I counted out her $50 in change, two 20's and a 10. It wasn't until after the women had left the van that I realized they'd also picked up the $100 bill. Fifty dollars in free tours, $50 in change plus their original cash. Not a bad profit for their morning.

I called their hotel and a few local businesses, to warn them and also to reassure myself I was not the only sucker. And I'm still not sure what happened. I remember the white peasant blouse. I remember losing $50 in cash at a time when every dollar counted. The rest is a blur.

Not everyone trusted me, either, even when I offered something free. Nearly everyone who came to live in Alaska by choice rather than birth has a story to tell about why and how. And they remember the precise date they arrived. The anniversary date of my arrival in Alaska was August 13. It was a Friday, it was raining, it was in Anchorage. I spent my first night in a questionable downtown motel with no lock on the door. We tend to remember such details. Now, August 13, 1985, was my 20th anniversary. I decided to celebrate by offering free tours on that day and wrote "Free Tours" on my eraser board sign. When people stopped I'd explain the reason behind the offer. Not one person accepted a free tour from me that day.

Ever searching for a gimmick to set my tours aside, I came up with another idea to attract attention. I offered one free tour by drawing. I'd collect the money at the glacier, I explained, and I'd do a drawing with the winner getting a free tour. My passenger load that day included three couples. At the glacier I proceeded with my new idea, and the men protested they thought the whole tour was free. I apologized for the misunderstanding, but the look on their wives' faces told me they understood perfectly well. They probably go to restaurants and complain about the food to get a free meal, I thought. Nevertheless, it was a one-day idea I abandoned in short order.

And there was another time I had three couples—what is it about the number three? They said they were in no hurry and I enjoyed their company so I extended my usual route, going out North Douglas Island for some of my favorite coastal views and photo sites. At some point when the tour was in overtime one of the women complained about fumes. I didn't notice anything; my van was routinely inspected and cleaned daily. There was something about the way she kept after it that aroused my suspicion about her motives. I kept my nose in overdrive the rest of the day but never picked up on anything wrong. To my relief she didn't come back to me and complain again.

We were running tours pre-cell phone, of course, something unimaginable today. Ever mindful of a possible emergency, Blue and I tried to communicate with each other by CB radio phones, but our efforts were mostly thwarted by mountains that blocked the signal.

Rarely did our passengers have another tour booked after ours. Our main deadline was getting them back to the dock in time for their designated meal hour. Dinners were served in one of two sittings, and arriving late was not an option. Though we tried to keep our tours on schedule, Blue and I also liked to make people feel they were getting a little something extra.

Late one afternoon I was returning downtown via Twin Lakes, a residential area along two small lakes that separated the old highway from Egan Expressway. Before the lakes were created by construction of the expressway, Blue's husband had set power poles along the shore by helicopter at low tide. We stopped for a photo and when I turned the key to restart the van, nothing happened. I turned the key again. Nothing. And again, nothing. It was after 6 p.m., and most tours were over for the day. Taxis that were usually everywhere were nowhere to be seen. Office buildings were closed, and I needed a phone badly.

This time more than dinner was at stake. I had a passenger from one of the few ships at that time that catered to people with special medical needs. He was on dialysis, and his next appointment was scheduled at 7 p.m. Somehow I found a building still open though mostly deserted a few blocks away, located a pay phone and called a taxi to get my passengers back to the dock on time. When cell phones became available, I was one of the first in line.

At least twice in one of those early years we saw cruise ship travelers with both legs amputated. They didn't have artificial legs, they didn't sit in wheelchairs. They simply ended mid-thigh, resting and moving themselves about on small wooden platforms that reminded me of plant stands on wheels. One wore a top hat, and gray suede leather gloves that protected his hands as he pulled along the sidewalk to move around. Neither Blue nor I had one of these men as passengers, but one signed up for flight seeing, which people reached by van ride to the aircraft. The van driver was clearly uncertain how to approach the double amputee, finally lifting the man under his armpits into the vehicle after asking if that was okay. I watched his discomfort, and wondered how I would have handled the situation. But mostly I was in awe of people with courage to travel under such odds, when it would have been so easy to just stay home.

8. It's All Outdoors

"Why do you want to go to Alaska?" a perplexed friend asked Alaska-bound visitors from Lawrence, Kansas. "It's all outdoors."

As in other places, Alaskans have built enclosures to fend off cold and rain and snow. But what happens beyond their confines seems to inordinately shape and define our lives whether indoors or out.

One of the first upgrades on my van, after the speaker system, was variable speed windshield wipers. It was clear early on that manually operated wipers with two speeds, on and off, weren't up to their task.

Thanks to orographic lift, it rains a lot here. Warm, moist air masses from the Pacific lift up over the Coast Range behind us, cooling as they climb and dropping on us the moisture they can no longer sustain in their grasp.

"Rain fills the salmon streams and grows glaciers," I'd remind my passengers, adding "You don't get lush forest in a desert."

Most of them enjoyed the rain, too. Coming often from the hot, arid American Southwest or the hot, humid Southeast, they found this a welcome change. For those who were not mollified, I'd remind them "You get to go home. We are home."

Still they were genuinely puzzled by our deep affection, even preference, for cool, dewy weather. We embrace misty watercolor days when mountain and sky blend seamlessly. When I moved here in pre-digital days, I used a 35mm camera and thought its light meter was broken. How could it be so dark? I wondered. Light that was not sponged up by slate skies was grasped by looming mountains. You could take a photo with color film, have the roll developed and swear your camera must have been loaded with black and white film instead.

"Some days all the color just leaves," my husband told friends in states painted in brighter hues.

"Don't you get depressed?" they'd ask. A reasonable question, in a place where on nearly any given day the odds are better it will rain than it won't, and yearly totals add up to more than seven feet of moisture. We are mainly creatures of light, and sunny beaches understandably beckon countless visitors. Truthfully, the rain never depressed me. Endless gray days when nothing happens, yes. But rain is a happening.

Ours is rarely a heavy, pelting rain. Here the rain is uncommonly gentle, silvery, light to the touch. Is it raining? Often we barely notice, unsure if at some given moment it's raining or not.

When the sun reappears after a protracted rainy spell, it is undeniably euphoric, a high without sniffing, poking or swallowing. Surreal, even. We wear a helpless smile that we're powerless to erase. That's on days one and two. By the third day, or definitely by the fourth, an edgy restlessness creeps in. The northern sun can have a hard brassy edge. Then a moodiness follows, making us downright unpleasant. "Where is the rain?" we begin to ask. When overcast skies and a gentle mist return, we breathe deeply and sink into the safety of a warm hug. Once again, our world is operating as it should.

I held an umbrella (red of course) so often those first few years on the street that it became a signature along with red rubber boots. Finally I hung a cloud-shaped sign from one of the ribs with red lettering that read "Tours."

Monday, July 16, 1984, brought heavy rains, 1.35 inches in 12 hours at the airport. That doesn't sound like much. In more horizontal places it might clog drains and flood streets. Here the rains and strong winds loosed tons of mud, debris and trees on Thunder Mountain and sent them coursing down in a frenzied mass that damaged a small hydro dam, two homes, a barn and a veterinary clinic. A river 30 feet wide continued to flow down the hillside more than an hour after the initial slide.

For several years I'd point out the growing ugly brown gash from Douglas Island across the channel, a few miles away.

A decade later, a family who owned a landscape and nursery business in the Mendenhall Valley began to transform the scar. They purchased surrounding land and set out to restore a stream wiped out by the slide. Ponds with waterfalls were installed, rhododendrons and azaleas and Japanese maples were planted, baskets of flowers were hung from the roots of upside down tree stumps. Golf carts now carry visitors up the mountain on a path created by the slide. The unsightly slash transitioned into a 50-acre botanical garden that now hosts weddings, parties and tourists.

The North Pacific Current, which we often call the Japanese Current, is a slow, warm water current that flows west to east, giving Southeast Alaska a moderate maritime climate with cooler summers and warmer winters than northern inland states. Our total temperature swing, on average, is pretty small. When I first moved to Juneau in October, I thought of 40 degrees as our generic temperature.

Had our outdoor thermometer broken in the move from Anchorage, I wondered? It seemed to read 40 degrees every morning, mid-day and evening. This wasn't a place to swelter by day or shiver by night. It was a place where long sleeves felt good most of the time. How many turtlenecks have I gone through over the years? Hard to say, but they've been a mainstay since I stepped into a cool August day in Anchorage and happily discovered wool wasn't just for winter anymore.

When I planned custom itineraries, I often advised travelers from the Upper Midwest and East Coast to dress for October.

"How cold does it get here in the winter?"

It was the predictable first question as people settled into their seats in my van and we began the ascent of the hilly downtown streets.

Were they testing me?

Well, I was ready. I welcomed it. I could say from experience, not a three-ring binder of crib notes, what it was like last winter, and the one before that, and the one five years ago. I was proud, all right, a tad arrogant, that I wasn't one of those outside college students the big tour companies liked to recruit on Pacific Northwest campuses and train as drivers near their bus barns. "Gray tours," I and my fellow independent tour operators sniffed, dropping the last half of the name of the largest bus tour operator.

You can teach drivers on-board narration, one of their managers told me, so long as they could thread a 40-passenger bus through downtown Juneau's narrow hilly streets.

Through the years the big companies bowed to community pressure and economic expediency, turning to local hire for their driver/tour guides, but back in 1984 nearly all were imports.

Weather is a big part of what it means to be in Alaska. The air here has a different quality, a different texture when you rub it between your fingers. Somehow it feels richer and thinner at the same time.

Fog that limits air travel to wings with feathers, winds that leave you gasping for air, heavy rains and snows that turn mountainsides into chutes for mudslides and avalanches—these tend to draw a border around your day. Except for some fog, visitors wouldn't experience most of them in summer.

One foggy morning I headed toward the glacier, along with the usual fleet of tour buses and taxis. We could have been in Florida. There wasn't a mountain in sight, the glacier had vanished. I decided to wait it out a bit with my passengers, who indulged my optimism and my patter about the virtues of mystery. Gradually a slight tear appeared in the curtain of fog on the far right hand side of the glacier. It grew larger and rounder until there was a porthole extending from the top of the face of the glacier to the point where it met the water. Then it suddenly opened to reveal the entire face, like gift wrapping torn asunder. My passengers gasped. Could I resist pointing out that if they had taken a bus instead of my tour, they would have left before the fog lifted to keep a predetermined schedule? I could not.

In 2000, as cruise ships turned south for the year in late September, fog settled firmly over Juneau and lingered longer than anyone could remember. These were not fog banks that swallow you up, and then release you. No, this was a blanket without seams, a down coverlet with no edges, as impenetrable as a bottle of milk.

Heavy fog continued with copious October rain, in a month when rain reliably transitions from light mist to heavy downpour. Our single commercial jet airline had installed navigational equipment to allow landings and take-offs with one-quarter mile visibility—a mere 1,300 feet—but still no flights could land for three days. Hundreds of passengers were stranded. By the end of the month eight tons of incoming mail was stockpiled in Sitka just 15 minutes away by jet. Outgoing mail was not going anywhere.

At first it felt cozy in a curl-up-with-a-book-by-the-fireside sort of way. Our world assumed an air of inscrutability. We knew mountains were all around us, we just couldn't see them. Local meteorologists blamed it on the warmer-and-wetter-than-normal weather. Instead of moving to colder and drier winter weather, our typical fall weather tarried into December.

In Southeast Alaska we typically see 20 to 35 days a year when fog dominates, actually less than along the Washington, Oregon and Northern California coasts, where 60 to 80 days a year are foggy. But this just seemed unacceptable.

When clouds finally lifted off the ground after what seemed like months, and the contours of our world came back into view, we felt liberated. And suddenly the fog felt oppressive in a way we didn't even know we felt.

The summer of 1999 was another story. On June 9, a helicopter pilot navigating by sight in whiteout conditions was unable to distinguish between low clouds and featureless snow-covered mountains and glacier. Flying blind and momentarily disoriented, he steered himself and six passengers into a mountain. No one survived. On July 27 a small cruise ship struck a rock in upper Tracy Arm while viewing tidewater glaciers and began taking on water. On August 4 a small cruise ship and a state ferry nearly collided in heavy fog in Peril Strait.

Then on September 10, three helicopters with 19 people were stranded atop a glacier through the following morning. The first chopper hit the glacier hard and turned over in disorienting white-out. A second helicopter sent to check on the first one rolled over on landing. The third one picked up occupants of the second and was en route to the site of the first when it rolled over, too. By midnight 19 people were gathered in two locations on the glacier in sub-freezing weather, including a nine-member Coast Guard rescue team. This time the outcome was better than in June; the main casualties were sore ribs, sore legs and a broken ankle.

Helicopter tours are a mighty source of cash for the cruise industry. They are among the priciest and most popular shore excursions. Cruise ships get a healthy commission for the tours they sell in port stops, which is why passengers hear a lot about them from the time the ship sets sail.

On August 1, when the local Sunday paper ran a major front-page story on flight safety concerns, every copy was removed from every newspaper box a tourist might conceivably walk by in the downtown area. The display copy was purchased for $1.25 to open the rack, the rest were simply stolen. All copies mysteriously disappeared, dumped in the channel, perhaps, or the landfill. It's hard to say, but no clue was ever announced about the whereabouts or the perpetrators.

The same thing happened in July, after the fatal flight-seeing helicopter crash in June. All copies of papers were removed from the downtown corridor, with just 50 cents for one copy of the weekday daily left behind in each stand. Did someone simply not want tourists to read about flight-seeing crashes or flight safety issues, a newspaper editorial asked?

It was yet another reminder that by the late 1990s, local tourism was firmly in the heady realm of big business.

Winter winds–we call them Takus for the glacier–blow mainly October through March. In those years when they occur, they torment the locals and those who come to town for the legislative session that opens in mid-January. Skies clear over Juneau as high pressure builds in the Yukon, behind the mountains that form the backdrop for Southeast Alaska. Mountaintop winds recorded at 200 miles per hour whip snow into vertical plumes hundreds of feet high, and create fuzzy white blurs that obscure the point where mountains and sky meet. They spill over the Juneau Ice Cap, sweep through downtown Juneau and save their greatest fury for downtown Douglas across the channel. Sustained winds of 30 to 50 miles per hour, with gusts exceeding 70 miles per hour, are the norm.

A Douglas couple with a waterfront home in direct path of Takus sweeping down from Mt. Roberts were celebrating their granddaughter's birthday in Hawaii around Christmas, 1996. Winds on the Douglas waterfront were clocked at more than 100 miles per hour when a Taku gust arrived with vengeance. It lifted the roof from their house and blew so hard it created a vacuum that sucked out all floor-to-ceiling windows in their frames, along with light-weight items like books, papers and cups. Some windows were tossed down onto the beach in front of the house, others flew completely over the top of the house and landed in the backyard. Furniture was jostled around but didn't fly away.

Unbeknownst to the owners, local contractors risked their lives in the midst of the maelstrom to climb onto the roof and tie it down with huge bands so wind couldn't take the rest of the house as well. During repair, windows were tied to the room with metal strips as a bulwark against future winds. The homeowners found pens, books, pictures, magazines, watercolor paints, brushes, shards of glass and other detritus in the backyard for years afterward.

As Taku winds rage downtown, the residential valley in front of the Mendenhall Glacier is typically dead calm. As you drive toward town on the daily commute, the first hint of winds begins beyond the valley walls, traveling past the flat open area of the airport. They pick up slowly until they pull against the car as it nears downtown. Getting out of a parked car during a Taku can be formidable. First you push the door open against wind, then you hold tight lest wind rips it from the hinges, while you gasp for breath in the outside air.

The closest I came to this feeling in a very different climate was on a late August trip to pre-Katrina New Orleans. After we had made flight reservations I began reading stories of other people who had unwittingly taken late summer trips to the Big Easy. But it was too late. Friends were already making plans for our arrival. No wonder, I thought later, our airfare was so cheap.

As a confirmed northerner, this was my first foray into the Deep South. We had a full itinerary. Beignets at the French Quarter. A walk around Lafayette Square. Muffuletta at Central Grocery on Decatur Street. Record heat and record humidity both stood at an even 100. The heat began as a warm embrace, pleasant and comforting. It quickly turned to an unyielding force, at the same time a brick wall and an animate being with a pulse of its own. I could not walk nor breathe; I was spent and powerless against it. Later I was struck how it felt strangely similar to railing against a Taku.

I have reached for signposts walking downtown Juneau in a Taku, feeling as if all 145 pounds of me would sail past plastic garbage cans in mid-air. Visitors who said they were searching for the real Alaska wouldn't have wanted this much reality.

Across from downtown Juneau, stops on Douglas Island offered another window onto outdoor Alaska.

I'd point out some of the more obvious avalanche chutes on Mt. Juneau and Mt. Roberts "in case we make the national news one day."

The article I most often cited was a 1982 story in *National Geographic* magazine which mentioned Juneau prominently, along with a color photo of a snow-dust cloud over downtown Juneau a decade earlier. It named Juneau the North American community most likely to have a major avalanche in the future

The angle of the slopes behind town (30 to 45 degrees), frequent fresh snow that fails to bond to a packed base, and alternating snow and rain all add up to unstable slabs of snow that can break free and move down slope at a speed that would garner a ticket on the Autobahn.

When avalanches travel the same path year after year, trees lack time to reassert themselves and set up a break wall. It's the more supple willow and alder that can bend with the stress of moving snow and wind and spring back, lending their bright green color to the slide areas. I'd also point out the homes built beneath them. When an avalanche and its blast of wind swept Mt. Juneau from top to bottom in the early 1900s, it did the heavy lifting of land clearing. We proceeded to build more than 60 homes, a hotel, a live-aboard boat harbor and the main road between downtown Juneau and the Mendenhall Valley in the lower reaches of its path.

Across the narrow Last Chance Basin from Mt. Juneau, Mt. Roberts climbs from sea level to its 3,819-foot summit in short order, mostly covered in thick forest of spruce and hemlock up to tree line. But here it's not solid forest, but forest interrupted. Nineteen avalanche paths empty onto Thane road, the most active of them above Suicide Falls.

The threat of avalanches over Thane Road, traversed daily by local residents, is not taken lightly. When the snow pack is deemed unstable, state highway employees aim a 105mm howitzer at snow fields high on Mount Roberts from about 2.3 miles away on Douglas Island. A projectile containing an explosive charge detonates on the rocks or hard snow. In January 1989 the detonation dislodged so much snow it cut off transmission lines from the hydroelectric plant that powers Juneau, and reshaped the lower route of Suicide Falls. The avalanche occurred during the strongest high pressure system recorded in North America, with unrelenting sub-zero temperatures and hurricane force Taku winds. A few days later, one of Juneau's two main back-up diesel generators failed. So here we were, nervously watching our power consumption at the most vulnerable time of the year, feeling our slender thread was perilously tenuous. City and state buildings were shut down overnight, half of the street lights were turned off, evening events were cancelled to save power. Pipes froze and the fire department was inundated with false alarms set off by high winds and low temperatures. It made a good story in the summers that followed, but the base of the falls seemed less photogenic and less appealing after that.

There was no shortage of other avalanche stories. One day my husband was driving down Thane Road to a business appointment when a mere shadow caught his attention. He instinctively accelerated the minivan in reverse just in time to see a wall of snow cross the road directly in front of him and charge halfway across Gastineau Channel. On the other side of the slide, heading back into downtown, a woman braked just in time to miss the avalanche.

In late February 1985 an avalanche rumbled down the west face of Mt. Juneau under cover of evening darkness. It came to rest a few feet above homes in its path, after snapping big trees and a telephone pole and piling against the side of a garage. It sounded to locals like a low-flying airplane or howling wind until they felt rumbling that proved otherwise.

A week later, a local avalanche expert was once again urging the city to buy out the most vulnerable homes before they were caught in the life-threatening avalanche he calls inevitable. After all, he pointed out, slides along the same snow slide zone reached tidewater in 1915 and 1926, and in 1962 a wind-borne avalanche ripped roofs and chimneys from several dozen homes. But local property owners resisted, and political will bowed to economics.

I loved stories like this the way comedians love government melt-down. They provided fodder for great dialogue, made me sound brave for living here, albeit not in the slide area, and left tourists thinking they were in an exotic locale on the precipice of danger, saved only by being here when mountainsides were devoid of snow.

The same day the local paper was quoting the avalanche expert's warning, it reported a 20-foot wall of snow had rumbled through Last Chance Basin behind the city, across the same road we drove taking summer visitors to the mining museum. It was the sixth avalanche in a week, blocking one of the caretakers at the museum, and giving pause to the other who'd walked that road into town two hours earlier. That wasn't the end of it. Just over a week later, at 5:30 a.m., another avalanche swept down Mt. Juneau, trapping a woman inside her two-story home with a 12- to 16-foot wall of snow. It blocked her first story windows, blew open a door, and started rolling snowballs into the house. And it was the second time her house had been hit in a month.

In spring when upper slopes are still covered with snow, you can see brown streaks of dirt and rocks carried down by sliding snow. But our tranquil summer tours gave little hint of winter's potential devastation.

9. Our Wild Side

Here where the human footprint is a smaller one, it is not only weather that forges our intimate relationship with the outdoors. Few things ignite our passions like wildlife.

In 1984 SeaWorld proposed to capture orca over a five-year period for temporary research and permanent captivity. They got a federal permit from National Marine Fisheries Service to capture 100 orcas, 90 for scientific study and release after two years, and 10 for captivity. The proposal was supported by the local newspaper and our lone congressman, but not by much of anyone else.

The response was greater than for any other issue of the day.

A group called Organized Resistance for Capture in Alaska, ORCA, gathered 6,000 signatures. The mayor of a local Tlingit community said, "Our people, we don't like to mess with nature; we feel we have a right to live free and the animals have that same right. These aren't killer whales you see at SeaWorld. Putting something in a cage, it makes it no longer what it is."

State legislators, deluged by mail, demanded a halt pending further study. Then-Governor William Sheffield asked the state

Department of Fish & Game to review the federal permit. The Sierra Club Legal Defense Fund filed suit. The SeaWorld spokesperson said, "We're still confident we can work this thing out."

"I've seen killer whale in action," our congressman Don Young said. "They'll go through a pod of seals like sickle through a wheat field and kill as high as 25 to 30 seals in one shot, cut 'em in half and turn around and have hors d' oeuvres. I don't think any Alaskans that have ever seen a killer whale in action have any compunction about them being captured...I just don't understand where this great concern over a predator ever occurred."

Within two weeks the governor asked the federal government to withdraw its permit, citing overwhelming opposition from residents.

If the issue of orca capture was short-lived, another wildlife controversy was not. Wolves, in particular, are as imbued with myth as with reality, and Alaskans are sharply divided. Wolves are such skilled predators that they can depress numbers of caribou and moose, particularly in harsh winters, leaving people who hunt for their food to harvest leftovers. Wolves don't rightly deserve all the blame, of course. Bear also add moose and caribou to their menu—as do subsistence, sport and trophy hunters.

In the 1940s and 1950s, federal agents lessened wolf populations through aerial shooting, poison and bounty payments. When Alaska won statehood in 1959, legislators promptly prohibited poisoning of predators and shortly stopped bounties. But private citizens took over aerial shooting where the feds stopped, with blessings of the state.

Over the years off-again on-again shooting, trapping, poisoning and sterilization have all been stirred into the mix. Ballot initiatives, legislative bills and executive actions cancelled each other out, one ignoring the other. In 1992 the Board of

Game endorsed wolf control in large areas of Interior Alaska, with state employees shooting wolves from aircraft.

As with the orcas, public outcry was immediate. The state received more than 100,000 letters of objection. A representative of a Bay Area nature preserve I'd been courting for a group tour to Alaska told me flatly she would not support travel to the state. Many small tour operators, the very ones who were philosophically opposed to wolf control, bore the brunt of cancellations from people boycotting the state. We were fodder for nightly national television.

The state scrapped shooting long enough to rename its management plan the Wolf Conservation and Management Policy and turn to trapping. Two years later video of a wolf in a snare brought more national publicity, all of it negative.

The debate, the initiatives persist. When a trapper took seven wolves on a Douglas Island beach across from Juneau in early winter of 2002, the response was again vociferous. Two adults, five pups were presumably the island's total pack, the first pack to be sighted there in two decades. Some people wanted to watch wolves, some wanted to protect the island's resident Sitka black-tailed deer for harvest. Policies for exterminating wolves to affect numbers of moose for hunters continue to divide Alaskans. Even in a state where harvest of game and fish is common and accepted, we have strong notions about when and how it should be done.

10. The Road South

The paved road south of town extends for seven miles before it abruptly ends, widening just enough for vehicles to turn around. Like the highway north, it too hugs the shoreline of Gastineau Channel, curving around the base of 3,819-foot Mt. Roberts.

This little stretch of road was one of my favorites. It was too narrow and too bereft of conspicuous attractions for sightseeing buses. Except for a few taxis, we'd have this stretch to ourselves, and my passengers could feel they saw something very few of their fellow travelers did. I hoped they would count it as bragging rights that night at dinner.

Waterfalls course over rocks just beyond road's edge all summer, fed by melt from snow patches at the highest reaches of Mt. Roberts. We often stopped in a small pull-out near the base of the largest, Suicide Falls.

"My husband proposed to me there," a local resident and volunteer in the visitor information booth for cruise ship travelers, told me. Exactly when and how the waterfall got the name Suicide Falls I never learned; it wasn't hard to imagine someone climbing rocks from the base of the falls high enough to hurtle down, but it wouldn't be an easy or sure end. I'd cautiously lead my passengers over rocks near the base, watching their every step, to take photos pointing up as water cascaded down. In early summer I'd identify the white thimbleberry and purplish pink salmonberry blossoms on bushes along the side of the stream. In August I would pick salmonberries and hand them to wary visitors.

"They're fine," I'd assure them, putting one of the raspberry-like berries into my mouth and swallowing it first.

"The salmonberries got their name because they're the color of salmon eggs," I'd tell them, offering the neon-orange berries that are longer on color than on taste. The red thimbleberries have a velvety texture that was less appealing to me, so I'd bypass them. This was my tour, after all, and I got to choose the berries.

For the wildflower photographers, I'd look for the red and yellow western columbine in bloom. Then we'd walk the shoulder of the road to a rocky stream that emptied under a flat bridge into the channel.

"I'm looking for a dipper," I'd explain.

Most people traveled north for showier species, and had never heard of the American Dipper, or Water Ouzel, as they were formerly called. But they willingly helped me scan the rocks for a nondescript, stocky little bird with an upturned tail. Its slate gray coloring blended neatly with rocks; what gave it away was movement, the constant bobbing up and down as it walked. Its nickname *dipper* likely comes from bending its legs so the entire body moves up and down in a dipping motion, though no one yet knows why these birds do the dipper bob.

A dipper might look plain, I'd tell them, but it's anything but ordinary.

Dippers are a most unlikely and unique combination. North America's only aquatic songbird, they sing, and they live in water. Find them along fast-moving mountain streams like this one, where they eat aquatic insects and small fish. They can swim with their wings, heads under water, turning over small rocks with their feet on the streambed in search of a caddisfly larva or sculpin.

Juneau biologist and author Mary Willson surveyed 40 streams to study local dippers. She and her assistants found 38 nests in 2005 and 44 nests in 2006. Mossy globes nearly the size of a volleyball, nests are typically built on cliff ledges next to a stream or behind a waterfall. If I had known about dipper nests in the 1980s, I would surely have tried to add a dipper nest to an eagle nest in my itinerary.

Dippers stay the winter when most song birds head south, inhabiting icy streams with sections of open water, glacial ponds, lakes, roadside ditches, and intertidal stream deltas. With their unusually dense feathers and heavy down, dippers bring unexpected song to a winter day.

They were John Muir's favorite bird, I'd say, though I can't be certain he'd put it at the very top of his list. He did write with great poetry of ouzel in the Sierras, their song through every season, every kind of storm, in concert with the stream itself.

More than any other writer, I liked to quote John Muir in my tours. I was always surprised when a passenger didn't know who he was, but I made sure they'd heard a bit about him before the tour was over.

Just seeing a dipper means a stream is healthy, I'd tell visitors. Dippers need unpolluted streams to reproduce and clear water to see their prey. The water in this stream looked clear, and I knew someone who had filled jugs of drinking water from this stream for years, though I wasn't one to recommend it. Even the clearest of streams can harbor Giardia, an unpleasant parasite that causes intestinal disease, cramps and diarrhea. "You never know what animal has done what in this water," I'd say if someone was inclined to cup their hands and take a drink.

As we continued our drive down to Sheep Creek I talked about the biology-challenged observers who named it on October 25, 1880. On that day Richard Harris and Joe Juneau, credited as Juneau's co-founders, killed several "mountain sheep" nearby. Harris, who lost out on having the city bear his name, wrote his account of the day and their naming of the creek along with the discovery of gold at Juneau.

If they'd been better biologists they'd have named it Goat Creek. Mountain goats live on rocky cliffs along coastal Alaska; Dall sheep are found in the dry Interior. But the name stuck.

We seem to have an innate curiosity about how places were named, and people often asked about the source of Juneau names. This was a place to talk about dreams won and lost, and the man for whom this road was named, Bartlett L. Thane.

The once-upon-a-time community of Thane was centered here around the eve of World War I: a half-dozen boarding houses, some 50 homes, a general store, school, meat market, bakery, gymnasium clubhouse, and 11,000-volume library. Thane was promoter and general manager of the Alaska Gastineau Mining Company, a highly successful milling operation at Sheep Creek. The company's engineers were world famous for their feats; the mill set world records for high-volume, low-cost milling. But its ore was too low grade to generate a profit. The mine closed in 1921, just a decade after it was incorporated. Thane died broke and broken six years later of pneumonia, at the age of 49. All that remains is his name, and mine tailings dumped along the beach.

Today tourists eat fresh halibut and salmon at a cookhouse built in the style of an old mess hall atop those tailings. When Blue and I later catered to groups it was our restaurant of choice for its rustic atmosphere, out of the way location, fresh seafood, and a chance to pan for gold in the tailings.

Early in the tourist season, through June, we'd drive down Thane Road only when time permitted, or if I thought it would be of special interest. We took builders past our nicest homes, found patches of wildflowers for photographers, added an extra dose of public art–sculpture, murals, totems–when people expressed interest. That was the luxury of our small group tours. Blue and I talked with our passengers and included stops geared to them.

11. The End for Which We Were Made

Starting in early July, I'd head my empty van two miles down Thane Road between tours to look for sign of the first returning salmon of the summer. I didn't have to look down, just up. When bald eagles started perching on spruce trees a short glide from water's edge, I knew the season of the salmon had come. It meant an end time for salmon, fast food for eagles. There would be a new stop to include on my tour.

Each evening after I'd cleaned and swept the van of vestiges of the day's passengers, I'd check the tide table for the following day. Low tide was best. When low tide kept the salt water at bay, we could walk along the rocky beach right next to fresh water rivulets filled with salmon, following along as they pushed against the current in streams so shallow the fish were half out of water.

Like most things worthwhile, the observation takes a bit of focus. A salmon stream is an unfolding discovery. "I don't see anything," visitors would say with a trace of frustration.

First your eyes see just a dark shadow. Then a movement will catch your attention, maybe a single dorsal fin slicing through water.

"There's one!" they'd say. Then they'd see another fish, and then another as their eyes grew accustomed to what to look for. Wildlife watching is like that, knowing when and where to look, how to listen, even what to smell. The time for spawning varies by location of the stream and the species, but once you'd learned nature's calendar, sightings were pretty much guaranteed. Few wild creatures are as accessible as spawning salmon.

"I've seen it on television," they'd say. "I never imagined it would be like this."

The frenzied movement seems to defy physics itself as the salmon push upstream in staggering numbers. You wonder how they can move against each other, never mind against the power of water flowing down while they are swimming up.

Seeing it through the lens of her daily life, Wendy from Washington, D.C., said "It looks just like the Beltway."

At the peak of the run, streams are seething with a life force that belies what will follow. Soon these salmon, having insured a new generation and spent their last vestige of energy, will all be dead.

My ad for photography tours landed Wendy in my van. Brown-haired and square of face, she had come alone for a week to celebrate her 36th birthday. It was July, and I took her to the salmon stream at low tide. Each day I'd take her to another of my favorite photo spots. We went to a cove at Auke Lake brightened with butter yellow spatterdock water lilies. We walked Outer Point Trail on North Douglas Island, through muskeg, past a long-abandoned beaver pond, and onto the rocky beach with tidal pools. We visited the small log Presbyterian chapel with clear glass altar windows overlooking lake and glacier that brought gasps from the most jaded of tourists. Each day she asked to return to the spawning salmon.

It was nearly always this way. There is only so much scenery you can absorb before the mind drifts to the more mundane.

But when we got to the salmon spawning streams in midsummer it was hypnotic.

I would begin the story of the salmon. "Natives called them 'the swimmers.' "

The swimmers. That pretty much says it all. There's music in finding the core of a thing, stripping it of the non-essentials.

"Pacific salmon spawn only once. The female moves gravel with her tail to make a nest, called a redd. She lays the eggs, and a male swims beside her to release milt to fertilize them," I explained, going on to tell them how the female salmon uses her tail again to cover the fertilized eggs with gravel. And how she moves upstream to make another nest, maybe four or five times, until all the eggs have been released.

"Do they have contact with each other?"

A good question, and a frequent one. They went through an awful lot of trouble to reproduce if they couldn't have a few moments of pleasure before they died. Darned if I knew.

The eggs are neon orange and easy to spot, a gift for a tour guide. I'd point out little clusters of eggs caught in the stream bed. It helped bring the cycle to life. Some of the eggs float away, never to hatch at all. Some will be eaten by the Dolly Varden that haunt salmon streams to feed on the eggs. "Of the millions of eggs that are laid, very few grow up to be salmon," I'd say. More than 40 species–count us among them–feed on salmon eggs, juvenile fish, live adult salmon or their carcasses. The salmon that have survived fishing nets and hungry eagles, overcome beaver dams and navigated natal streams with too little or too much water long enough to spawn are something to admire.

All Pacific salmon hatch in fresh water, spend part of their life in the ocean and then return to the same fresh water stream to spawn.

"These are pink and chum," I'd say. No one would say these are the glamour species. Of the five species of Pacific salmon, you'd never hear someone say, "I'm going fishing for chum," or "Gee, I hope I hook a pink." Such aspirations are reserved for Chinook, also called kings. It's no surprise that bigger is better in the domain of fishing, and kings tug hardest on the scale. Even in technical government fisheries reports, pinks and chums seem to go to the back of the booklet like an afterthought.

The five species each have at least two nicknames, which I struggled to recall, and the Latin name I couldn't pronounce, let alone remember. Chum, also called dog salmon, are a mainstay for people in the Arctic and Interior Alaska, but sport anglers here catch them on the way to something else. Their giant eggs are prized as roe for people inclined to that delicacy. Pinks, or humpies, are bread and butter to local communities, but they weigh in at a lightweight five to six pounds at best. Coho, or silver, are prized sport fish because they put up the biggest fight and whirl through air and water with the grace worthy of Cirque du Soleil. Sockeye, or red, have red flesh that makes them the favorite of those who get their fish from a can.

Chinook is the king, the object of every sport angler's desire. It's the state fish, the biggest in every way. Just an ordinary catch can exceed 30 pounds. The record, unbroken since 1986, was a 97-pound fish taken up north (the term Southeasterners use for the rest of the state) in the Kenai River. Taking my daily dialogue from the local newspaper, I duly reported the catch when it happened as another item of news of the day.

"They leave the stream where they hatched to enter the ocean. Depending on the species and the fish, they'll spend between one and seven years in the ocean," I'd continue. Pinks may stray no more than 150 miles from the mouth of their home river before coming back to spawn after a year at sea. Kings may travel 2,500 miles from their home stream and stay at sea four to seven years before coming back to spawn. The distances exceeded my imagination.

I liked to recite such detail, but it didn't seem to matter as much to my passengers. There were long pauses when people seemed content to just watch in silence, adrift in thoughts beyond my reach.

"How do they know where to come back?" It was another frequent question. How little we still know about the creatures who share our planet.

For salmon, it's seemingly the sense of smell that brings them back to the stream of their birth. Even for us, a scent so interweaves distant memories. A certain disinfectant brings me back to our honeymoon hotel in Acapulco. Jean Naté cologne transports me to a Midwest college dorm where all the freshman girls were wearing it.

But in this case, it's an overarching memory of home. Salmon return to the stream where they were hatched by remembering the smell of that stream. Soil and decaying plants and animals give each stream its own distinct smell. Some researchers think it's even more complicated than that, that salmon use some combination of the earth's magnetic field, celestial navigation, patterns of polarized sunlight and instinctive patterns of movement along the continental shelf to arrive back in the home neighborhood. It's hard to imagine fish looking up at the stars, but they looked up at us along the streams, so who's to say it isn't possible.

I'd also quote Henry Beston, who spoke of our fellow creatures far better than anyone else I know of in his classic, *The Outermost House*. "We need another and a wiser and perhaps a more mystical concept of animals. . . .in a world older and more complete than ours they move finished and complete, gifted with extensions of the senses we have lost or never attained, living by voices we shall never hear." Once salmon get close to their natal stream, smell takes them home.

"After they spawn, they all die," I'd go on.

"Even the males?" It was usually a man who asked.

"This is an equal opportunity activity. They all die."

Males have perhaps the harder time of it. Before returning to fresh water to spawn, some develop a bizarre hump in their back, most pronounced in the pinks, which earned the nickname "humpies" for good reason. Some develop sharp canine-like teeth and you can see flesh nipped out of the backs of some males where they've fought to insure the strongest will leave their DNA to the new generation.

Salmon stop eating when they return to fresh water, and the change in color means they are feeding off their own body fat reserves, I'd explain. Sockeye turn bright red as they return to fresh water, making them a favorite of photographers. They are the species with starring roles in the travel brochures.

"These salmon have it easy," I'd assure them as we looked down upon the stream. Their distance from salt water to fresh water spawning grounds is in some places mere yards. In other parts of the Northwest salmon push hundreds of miles upstream, against strong currents and rapids, to reproduce. Yukon River spawners bound for headwaters in the Yukon Territory travel more than 2,000 miles over two months.

As the season progresses, the live salmon thread past carcasses of earlier spawners strewn across the rocky beach. Some are still gasping, maybe by reflex. Some have gaping holes where their eyes once watched for passing food, insects and zooplankton. The shiny eyeballs are a favorite of the ravens, who sometimes pluck them out while the fish are still alive.

It got more grisly as the weeks passed. While the streams we followed along the beach had natural runs, the numbers of fish were inflated by a salmon hatchery just across the road. When salmon returned in great numbers, college students home for the summer donned stained yellow rubber overalls to gaff fish from the holding tanks that the hatchery-bred fish had spent their last energy to reach. They sorted them by sex and species, milked the milt and slit the bellies of females to remove eggs.

The milt and eggs would be stirred together in a bucket to produce the smolt that would start their ocean voyage the next spring. It was an unseemly end for one of nature's epic journeys.

Northern visitors came to "see" wildlife. "Open all your senses," I'd tell people. No one missed the point here amid all those decaying bodies. But within a surprising few weeks even the overwhelming odor begins to dissipate, along with nearly all traces of the salmon.

"Does someone clean them up?" I was often asked.

In our take-charge world it's hard to imagine a place where our involvement really isn't needed.

"Yes," I'd say. "We call in the clean-up committee. The ravens, eagles, gulls, bear. Soon nearly every trace is gone."

"It's so sad," someone would usually say. Here I'd recount one of my favorite novels. A young Indian woman came to a salmon stream, just like this one, I'd say, and tears came to her eyes. "The end of the swimmer is sad," said the girl on the brink of womanhood. But a young vicar who'd come to her village saw something else.

I quoted the vicar's words. "The whole life of the swimmer is one of courage and adventure. When the swimmer dies he has spent himself completely for the end for which he was made."

I'd pause. Then I'd ask, "How many of us can say that?" People retreated into their own thoughts, and I'd tell them about the slim novel by Margaret Craven that I've read more times than I'm apt to admit. "It's called *I Heard the Owl Call My Name*. You can get it at the bookstore downtown," I'd say. "It's a beautiful story about life and death and beauty and everything that matters in life. It's set in a Native village in British Columbia, but it's a place a lot like this one."

If I could write something that touched other people as much as that book touched me, my own life would be a success, I'd think to myself. Though we are prone to divide books into fiction and non-fiction, it is often in fiction that we can bear to hear the truth.

Here the salmon were telling their own story, and people couldn't turn away. This was the stop on my tour where everyone wanted to linger, when returning to the cruise ship for the first dinner seating mattered least.

Sometimes a trip seems too much to absorb at the time. Once we've returned home and worked through the transition of paperwork and daily routine, it becomes more vivid and clear. The most memorable parts float to the top and become deeply etched in our minds. For those who come to Alaska during the season of the swimmer, I wonder how many carry that as the memory that lingers.

"What is the best time to come?" many Alaska-bound visitors ask. I recite the litany of things I treasure most in this corner of the far north. That bright chartreuse of new spring growth, as willow and alder unfurl their leaves in our mostly coniferous forest. The Arctic nesters stopping off to feed on their annual spring migration travels. The resident hatching eaglets, song sparrows, harlequins. New Sitka black-tailed deer, baby mountain goats. All reasons to come in May. In June, shooting star, lupine, baby seals on ice floes, endless days of summer solstice. Spawning salmon and bear watching in July. Wild berries in August. Further north, the magic of late August, early September when tundra turns red and gold, animals sport their richest coats, northern lights return to blackened skies, and Denali, the continent's highest peak, emerges from the clouds it spins in summer.

The next time someone asks, I will simply say "Come in July."

12. The Place Where No One Died

One summer I took a class called A Sense of Place at Chautauqua Institution in western New York. It explored how we relate emotionally to a particular place, whether that place is a landscape, a place of worship we count sacred, a place we've journeyed or a place we call home. I speculated that all of us in Alaska have a drawer full of Alaskan tee-shirts and sweatshirts. None of my classmates, from a cross-section of other states, owned a tee-shirt reflecting their home area.

"How long have you lived here?" visitors often asked me.

"Nineteen years. Thirteen years up north; six years here." That was my answer in 1984.

"Do you like it?"

Maybe some people could live 19 years in a place they did not like. I am not one of them.

What they really meant, I think, was "Why on earth do you live here?" Or, more likely, "How can you stand it?"

"We talked about it and we said it's a beautiful place to visit, but we can't imagine why anyone would want to live there," said a friend and life-long resident of rural New York after a week-long visit.

Truthfully, I didn't know the answer myself. People who've lived here for years, who wouldn't for a moment entertain thought of life anywhere else, are still hard-pressed to explain why. Few of us can assimilate the sum of it, internalize it and distill its essence. Even artists and poets, those we look to when our own words founder, often fall short

We are still waiting for our Van Gough or Monet to give voice to the beauty that overwhelms us—for a Tennessee Williams to articulate our northern desires.

The soul of a place is in its minutest details. Laurie, a local artist, naturalist and environmental activist, walked the same mile-long trail along the Mendenhall Wetlands every day for more than 20 years, through rain above, ice under foot, biting winds, even rare wilting heat. She names the eagles and witnesses their courtship and mating, watches an eaglet lift a fuzzy head and take its first tenuous flight, follows the trails river otters leave in snow. She records the spring day when worms first appear on the dike trail and proclaims it "Worm Day," notes the blossoming of fireweed in summer and the gossamer seeds that cling to red-and-gold-leafed fireweed stalks in fall. Could she do the same thing through the tall grass prairie in Kansas or the Great Dismal Swamp in Virginia? Probably, but it is impossible to imagine her separate from this place where she has lived so intently that she and the place have become one.

On Rachel Carson's 100th birthday, a day after witnessing a spectacular calving at Mendenhall Glacier, Laurie began an email with a quote from Carson: "What if I had never seen this before? What if I knew I would never see it again?"

Richard Nelson, a celebrated nature author from Sitka who's struggled with the question of "Why here?" for years, came closest to an answer, I think. He said, "It is the sheer wildness of this place." Enclaves of people and civilization surrounded by wildness that pulls at a primal force deep within.

Many of the visitors Blue and I met were from the Atlantic Seaboard, and I'd try to think of parallels they could relate to. "In the East you have pockets of wildness surrounded by centuries-worth of development," I'd say. "Here there are pockets of development, surrounded by wildness." It would be a mistake to say "untouched." Earlier peoples have lived and moved freely through these environs well before Alexander the Great was conquering his known world.

A young man moved from a frontier town in the Yukon to Vancouver, British Columbia. When I first saw Vancouver I thought it as perfect a city as I'd ever seen. Punctuated with stunning contemporary architecture, it had an international, cosmopolitan feel, but on a human scale. It was immaculately groomed, filled with parks and flowers. But for the young man, the perfection was its failing. It was the preciseness of a tulip garden, so orderly and flawless in every way, that did him in and sent him scurrying back to the frontier.

Most political boundaries bear little relationship to the geographical landscape on which they are imposed, and we have much in common with our Canadian neighbors in British Columbia and the Yukon. At a northern symposium, a speaker from a small Yukon town told his Juneau audience that no one used to die there. He meant that most people who lived there had immigrated from somewhere else, and when they died their bodies were shipped out to be interred in the place of their birth. Over time, the people who came there by choice rather than birth adopted the Yukon as a place to invest their soul. And when they died, they also chose to be buried there.

When I was about 30 it came to me that I too would die some day. When I flew Outside on family visits I would sometimes tremble through the entire flight. "What if I die while I'm outside of Alaska?" I thought. My obsession with this place ran so deep I was terrified of dying when I was away from it.

As one of Alaska's older non-Native communities, Juneau now runs four and five generations deep with two cemeteries in addition to Native burial grounds, plus a columbarium and innumerable cremated remains spread over wild places people loved in life. But throughout the state, it is still not unusual to live and die here, and be buried somewhere else.

13. Better Than a Beer

As we drove back into downtown Juneau I'd pick up some of the threads from the beginning of our tour. The glacier may give our community its identity, but the downtown waterfront is its heart.

As I leaned on the dock railing each day awaiting the first cruise ship passengers I had no clue what lay beneath the channel waters.

A piece of human skull with its jaw and gold bridgework still attached was found by a recreational diver on Halloween, 2001. Original analysis pinned time of death to more than a few weeks but less than a century. In January 2004 another piece of human skull was found in the muddy bottom near Marine Park, feeding rumors both pieces were remains of the same local man pulled beneath channel waters by a giant squid in July 1956.

In March 2004, more remains of a human skull were found. It's not hard to imagine sliding into the waters from shore on a dark Juneau night. Passions and tempers flare. Relationships turn. Alcohol numbs the senses. People glide easily into the depths, unheralded and unaccounted for.

"Diving is better than a beer after work," says Annette, who found all the remains. "Six feet under and you're completely separated from work on top," which in her case was the high stress world of a supervisor and computer programmer. She started diving in Fiji at the age of 45. "It was curiosity that got me there," she says. That, and a lot of grit. After nearly drowning in a canoe at 18, even standing under a shower "freaked me out," she said. Inquisitiveness and sheer will prevailed. After a lot of premature surfacing, she finally overcame her past, and now says she "gets grumpy" if she doesn't get under water regularly.

She's dived 233 feet into the sea, watched a 500-pound halibut bend its head back to its tail. She's seen purplish giant squid egg sacs free-floating and undulating like a daydream, and seen monster sponges six feet across by 10 feet high.

Human remains aren't the only things she found mired on the bottom of the channel, out of sight for the sleek cruise ships that maneuver above and their passengers. She's found credit cards, phone cards, cruise ship ID cards, mountains of beer bottles, a "Vote Here" sign and lots of "adult sippy cup lids," the lids from disposal coffee cups.

I wish I'd known these stories when I had passengers to share them with.

People often asked about the flags lining the downtown route. In 1977 a call went out urging people to buy a state flag. Rudy Ripley, the commercial artist who painted the signs on my van that made it my own, spearheaded a project to fly flags from all 50 states on light poles leading into downtown Juneau. "Buy the flag from your home state," was the mantra, as many Alaskans still move here from somewhere else.

As we drove along, I'd invite people to look for their own home state flag, telling them it was likely funded by a Juneau resident who grew up there.

A lot of the state flags are blue, and alike in their rainy limpness. Only in the stiff breeze of a storm do they unabashedly proclaim their identity, standing straight at attention with every seal and stripe and border clearly revealed. To help their search, I'd say "You can look for the postal abbreviation on the pole." A lot of them didn't know what their flag looked like under the best of conditions.

But in Alaska nearly everyone knows the story of Benny Benson, part Russian-Aleut, part Swedish, sent to live in a boarding school at the age of four after his mother died. When he was 13, he entered a contest for Alaska schoolchildren to design a flag for the Territory of Alaska. Benny chose a dark blue background with eight gold stars, seven in the outline of the Big Dipper and one representing the North Star. Most of

20. Flags

Flags give you a good feeling. When I vacationed on the German island of Norderney in the North Sea my cousin flew an American flag in welcome. He has flags from many countries and when someone visits he flies their country's flag.

Alaska's flag, with gold stars on a deep blue background.

the hundreds of entries reflected just one aspect or region of the vast territory; Benny's clean elegant design encompassed them all. The original, made of blue silk and appliquéd gold stars, was first flown on July 9, 1927. When Alaska became a state in 1959, the flag endured, its symbolism enshrined in Alaska Statutes:

> The design of the official flag is eight gold stars in a field of blue, so selected for its simplicity, its originality, and its symbolism. The blue, one of the national colors, typifies the evening sky, the blue of the sea and of mountain lakes, and of wild flowers that grow in Alaskan soil, the gold being significant of the wealth that lies hidden in Alaska's hills and streams.
>
> The stars, seven of which form the constellation Ursa Major, the Great Bear, the most conspicuous constellation in the northern sky, contains the stars which form the "Dipper," including the "Pointers" which point toward the eighth star in the flag, Polaris, the North Star, the ever constant star for the mariner, the explorer, hunter, trapper, prospector, woodsman, and the surveyor. For Alaska the northernmost star in the galaxy of stars represents Alaska, the forty-ninth star in the national emblem.

As statutes go, this seems more poetic than most.

We usually crossed the bridge connecting downtown Juneau to Douglas Island, turning left toward downtown Douglas for views of downtown Juneau across the channel with cruise ships in the foreground and mountains behind. Many local names were bestowed by Captain George Vancouver in 1794. Douglas, I'd tell them, was named for John Douglas, Bishop of Salisbury.

I'd identify Gastineau Channel as we drove over the bridge, and someone usually asked who it was named for. I told them the origin was unclear; some guy would often bring up Mark Gastineau, New York Jets football player 1979 through 1988.

After crossing the bridge across Gastineau Channel, I most often just turned left to and drove two miles to downtown Douglas, once the largest city in the state and home to the world's largest gold mine. Flooding of underground mine tunnels and buildings in 1917 and a subsequent fire brought an end to that, and now most of its residents cross the bridge to go to work, while a few valley residents drive to Douglas for government jobs there.

Douglas is home to Perseverance Theatre, Alaska's flagship professional theater. Since its 1979 founding by Molly Smith, it has premiered more than 50 new plays and performed works by Tony Kushner, John Guare and Paula Vogel as well as Shakespeare. It set Macbeth in the local Tlingit culture, cast it with all Alaska Natives, and took it to the Smithsonian National Museum of the American Indian in Washington, D.C. It has imported and exported directors from New York and Washington, D.C.

21. The Chili Pot

The bar next to the Taku was the Billikin, owned by a former lady of the night, Elsie. Elsie and I became friends, exchanged bar customers and swapped booze. Elsie forever had a chili pot going. One night a fight started at the Taku while I was bartending. I pulled a 357 magnum from behind the bar; everyone stormed out and fled to the Billikin and across the street, to Louie's. The band kept playing "Johnny Be Good." Johnny, a kick-boxer, kept kicking left and right while playing his guitar. The bar closed early that night. Next day Elsie thanked me for not shooting through the wall at her chili pot. Years later, I had become a registered nurse's assistant in a nursing home in Juneau, and cared for Johnny as a patient/resident.

But all my passengers saw was a small blue awning from the outside. With most performances in fall and winter, the theater made barely a ripple in our tours. Before the building was converted to a theater, it housed the Taku Bar which Blue managed for four years.

The end of the road in Douglas leads to Sandy Beach, a remnant of the Treadwell gold mining operation that crushed tons of rock, separated the gold with mercury, and then dumped the left-over ground up rock along the waterfront. Sometimes Blue and I led visitors through old mine ruins along the beach, then up a steep hill to a glory hole, a deep hole simply abandoned after gold extraction ceased. I always watched uneasily as visitors peered over the edge into the abyss, littered with discarded automobiles pushed down to their final resting place. The car disposal stopped when someone realized that fluids from the junked cars were draining into the channel via old underground tunnels, I'd say.

"It's called a glory hole because if you lean too far over the edge, that's where you're going," I'd stress in my warning.

I thought this site would make a great setting for a murder mystery. What were the odds of ever finding a body disposed of here? Then I realized it would be an unsolvable crime. The body would never be found. No, it would take an Edgar Allen Poe to do justice to such a story.

Though downtown Douglas and downtown Juneau are a mere two miles apart by road, Douglas feels 50 miles away from the buzz of the cruise ship waterfront and the intrinsic tensions in offices managing the seat of government. On a rare sunny fall day I was walking along the Douglas small boat harbor when clarion voices traveled across the water: "You cross the bridge and people are different. They're just different."

When time allowed, I'd turn right at the Douglas side of the bridge. Douglas Island is about 14 miles long, eight miles wide at the widest point and tapering off to a point on the southern end. We'd follow the water north for about nine miles, past waterfront and upland housing developments, past roads to a heliport and to the uphill road to Eaglecrest ski area, stopping at a boat launch with great views of the Mendenhall Glacier across the channel, and possible sightings of eagles and even an occasional humpback whale. The road ends on the side of the island facing the mainland; it does not circle around to the other side. It was another end of the road.

14. Where I Learned to Sell Tours

Gradually I made the transition from selling two-hour sightseeing tours on the dock to planning and selling two-week itineraries. It wasn't in me to be less than honest with any potential client, though they had no way of knowing that. When I thought about it, I was in awe that people would send sizable checks to me, a small operator they knew nothing about. Part of it, I think, was the phone persona I developed in another job about the same time, where I learned to listen and to speak calmly with just about anybody.

The State of Alaska dispenses annual dividends from earnings on oil revenues to each of its residents. Most people who took a seat in my van had heard of the Alaska Permanent Fund and from the beginning I included it in my daily dialogue. Back then I'd say "The total account is worth about $23 billion; that's a 'b' for billion." They seemed impressed, but more interested in the fact that each October, every Alaskan got a dividend check. Paul Harvey liked to announce it on his noon radio show each year; he had a fondness for things Alaskan so it got widespread notice. I explained that at least 25 percent of revenues from oil production on the North Slope were placed in a permanent fund, with principal invested in stocks, bonds and real estate. Roughly half the earnings, based on a five-year average to account for ups and downs of investments, are distributed each year in the form of a dividend.

The dividends began in 1981, to protect public funds from politicians and give Alaskans a sense of ownership and commitment to their state. Alaska was and still is a revolving door, something not conducive to the financial, emotional and intellectual commitment that builds strong community. The dividend, thinking went, might encourage residents to think of Alaska as their permanent home. Over time people began to see the dividend as a birthright, not a bonus. They built it into their budget and when the check did not arrive as they expected, their response could be, well, explosive.

Alaskans have to submit an application each year during an open filing period and meet certain criteria to receive the dividend. In 1990 I got a winter job with the Permanent Fund Dividend Information Office, helping people apply and explaining the program requirements. It was a window on human nature unlike any I could have imagined.

"You'd think everyone would love you when you're giving away money," said the office supervisor with a hearty laugh during my job interview. We had an instant rapport and I knew the job was mine at the end of our interview. I also knew immediately what she was saying, though I would be surprised at the depth of that truth; nothing brings out our darker side like free money.

To qualify for a dividend, Alaskans have to be a resident for a year prior to applying and intend to remain an Alaska resident. They had to physically live in the state for most of the previous calendar year unless they were out on an allowable absence like college or medical treatment or military service. They can't do anything as a resident of another state, like get a divorce or vote or get resident college tuition. They have to fill out a form, answering questions all rife with potential for errors or downright falsehoods on their part. Computer keying errors on the state's part were also possible then; today most people complete their applications online and any keying errors are their own. Every year there'd be missing information that had to be supplied before the application was considered complete. Dividends were denied if people mailed applications the day after the deadline. And there were always applications that had to be reviewed by staff to determine if someone was eligible within the state statutes and regulations. Whole careers have been built around determination of eligibility for a permanent fund dividend.

To help people through the application process, the state set up information offices Alaskans could contact by phone or in person, or now by email. That was where my job came in.

From the anonymity of the telephone people would curse, lie, scream and cry. Free money has a way of laying people bare. Gentility can be a thin veneer, and people you'd least expect will shed any pretense of civility as readily as extra clothes on a warm day.

"I'm trying to call to see if I'm getting my #*# money," one call began.

There were days when I could feel the caller's hand reaching through the phone's mouthpiece and tightening around my throat. I would reach for my water bottle, listen, leave pauses unfilled for anger to dissipate and frustration to wane.

People confided the most intimate details of their lives if it would help insure their dividend. I heard about a sex change operation and subsequent change of name. "That's why the name on the birth certificate is different," the caller explained. I talked with mothers distraught when they learned their children's checks had been cashed and spent on alcohol by the children's father.

One caller was informed by letter that he wasn't receiving a dividend check because it was garnished.

"Who garnished my check?" he asked.

"Your check was garnished by Child Support," I read from his computer file.

"Wow. I just became a father. Now I just have to find out who," he said, sounding pleased at the prospect.

We talked with children too young to legally cash a check who were bearing children themselves. A day on the phone bank was exhausting. All of us went home at night with energy for little more than falling asleep in front of television.

"Can you tell me when my check was mailed?"

I looked up his record. "Your check has been cashed."

"How could she do that? We were just divorced. #*#." Click.

Callers didn't all swear, but clearly we were dealing with a subject that cuts pretty close to the bone: money. Supervisors told us we did not have to continue a conversation with someone who was swearing, but I always rode it out. If irate callers didn't hang up themselves, I felt good if I could calm them down and move forward.

Beyond the fatigue I loved the richness and breadth of all that humanity. Through it all I learned the calm, soothing demeanor, the reassuring air of confidence that would serve so well in selling my tour packages. If I could just get people to call me, and they were looking for the kind of service I offered, they were mine.

15. Saying Hello to New Friends

As I designed custom itineraries for independent travelers, I got to know my clients by phone and fax while planning their route. When I met them upon arrival in Juneau, holding a white erasable board with their name at the airport or ferry terminal, we felt like old friends. I no longer had to wear red to get their attention.

One day I was meeting a couple with the last name of Wolfe. They were optometrists, I learned from our numerous contacts in planning their trip. My "clever gene" went into overdrive. I found a cardboard mask of a wolf's head in a toy store, put sunglasses over the top and held it in front of my face when their flight arrived. A former co-worker who happened to be at the airport thought I'd regressed into total silliness until I explained to him later what it meant. But worst of all, my clients didn't recognize me because they didn't get it.

Tangible mementos of some visitors are scattered throughout my house as well as my memory. A satin-smooth hand-made walnut vase sits on my office bookshelf holding a matching walnut pen and pencil, all three a gift through two couples traveling together by RV. One of the errors I so regretted, and thus remember to this day, was failing to calculate the rental cost of their RV when quoting the original price of their trip. I priced out all itineraries on an Excel spreadsheet, and neglected to include the far right column in the AutoSum formula. I did not notice the mistake until well into the planning process, and it substantially increased the total price of their visit. I lamely blamed it on the computer; they were gracious in not pointing out the obvious: computers just do what we tell them to. The gift is a reminder of the forgiving man who made it in his home workshop and carried it north.

Some of my clients brought gifts at considerable inconvenience. People from Alaska and New Zealand seem to have a special affinity for each other. A couple from Christchurch not only lugged two bottles of local wine but later sent a three-page handwritten letter detailing the best time for me to visit their home area and offering to help arrange slide shows for potential Alaskan travelers. I was gifted with coffee table books from Brisbane and Tel Aviv—heavy, bulky additions to any luggage, never mind international travel half a world away.

A navy tee-shirt with a white satin lighthouse appliqué and "Great Lakes, Michigan," embroidered beneath it, was a gift from a spirited energetic solo traveler, an avid Red Wings fan from Detroit. There's "Old Bay" seasoning from Maryland, a reminder not only from the visitors who brought it, but also of the metal can that once sat on my mother's kitchen shelf.

My first unintended foray into itinerary planning was for a group of six travelers from greater New York City. They'd made arrangements on their own with a charter boat operator of colorful and questionable reputation, but I was asked for help in making reservations for Glacier Bay and activities around Juneau. Avid photographers, they taught me to see Alaska as a first-time camera-bearing visitor would see it. Through them I learned how it takes a day or two to calm down and focus inward before looking through the viewfinder.

"I don't know which way to look first," one said as we drove down Douglas Island across from Juneau. They saw vistas I'd overlooked in a decade of living here.

Weather during their visit was unusually rainy, with low flight ceilings. Flights were cancelled; it seemed that everything that could thwart and complicate plans did. They taught me how to deal calmly and reassuringly with the most demanding of clients, give credence to their feelings and turn them into long-time friends. I would come to see many times over that people will accept the annoyances and stress of travel if they are treated with respect, not patronized or demeaned or brushed aside. One member of the group, in particular, was my nemesis. I was so intimidated by brusque comments that I would later come to think of as just "so-New York" that I decided to cope by addressing everyone else in the group and ignoring him altogether. He was not deterred, and by week's end he was my favorite of them all.

After he returned home he'd send me calendars or magazines where I could submit my photos for publication and tips on where to advertise my business. A stock broker by trade, he'd also send me occasional stock tips though the market was not in my realm of thinking at the time. Although I didn't know where his office was located, in the aftermath of the Twin Tower bombings his was the name that came to my mind. On the fifth anniversary of 9/11, I brought myself to read the list of Trade Tower victims to see if I recognized any names, and it was his name, still fresh in my memory today, that I hoped I would not find. The list is alphabetized, and I had to go no further than the "G's" to reassure myself he was not among them.

By the early 1990s I'd made the full transition from hustling tours on the street to planning full itineraries for independent travelers. People who contacted me wanted to see Alaska on their own. They weren't inclined to cruise or sign on to a bus tour, but the logistics were just too confounding for two-career couples to find time to sort through.

Winter was my busiest time. People started making plans for the following summer around October. October was considered a watershed month; early bookings were the harbinger of a good season. The internet was not yet the resource it is today, and email wasn't in every household. It wasn't until 1993 that large network service providers America Online and Delphi started to connect their proprietary email systems to the internet. The White House went on line and businesses and the media began taking serious notice of the internet.

Much of our communication was still by telephone or fax. When the phone rang in early morning I sat up quickly thinking "East Coast," where callers often calculated Alaska time as later than their time rather than four hours earlier. I tried to pretend I wasn't in bed, I didn't work from a home office, and my clock didn't read 5 a.m.

We'd discuss what to include in their trip by phone, then I'd fax or mail a no-obligation itinerary for their consideration. They'd send a deposit; I'd send back brochures for the tours and housing I'd booked, along with brochures for the communities they'd visit. A few asked for references. I always volunteered references after that, proud that my itineraries were usually seamless and my customers were more than satisfied.

I wrote and designed my own brochures to send out as well, based on questions people often asked—what we now call FAQs. They received a packing guide, wildlife viewing tips, weather tips, and photo tips based on my own passion for outdoor photography. When I began hosting travelers from the United Kingdom it suddenly occurred to me that if an emergency befell someone from overseas, I would have not a clue what to do. Nor would I have fared much better in contacting the family for a domestic traveler, I realized. I created an emergency contact form that became a standard part of the mail-out package. Thankfully I never needed to use one, but it made me feel much better, and I think it reassured clients that I was concerned enough to gather the information.

Each traveler got a custom travel journal with their name and dates of the trip on the front cover and a page for each day listing date and day of the week, the main activity, and often a small photo or clip-art. There was room left for writing notes or thoughts, though I saw only one person who filled every bare space with handwriting.

Clients would also get a detailed daily itinerary folded into thirds so it fit into a business envelope, with accommodations, confirmation numbers, tour operators, schedules and contact phone numbers.

I was there to dispense advice, opinions and calm assurance, to be a steady voice in a far-off place, always accessible. My phone number was on every sheet of paper I'd send. "You can call me at any time during your trip," I'd assure them. After I started planning trips rather than just driving a tour van I didn't know exactly what to call myself, so I signed all my correspondence "Alaska Travel Specialist."

When my clients' itinerary brought them through Juneau, as it usually did, I was there at the airport or ferry terminal upon arrival, eager to meet them. After months of correspondence and phone calls, the thing I looked forward to most was meeting visitors face to face. When their itinerary did not bring them into Juneau I felt cheated.

In travel industry jargon, moving people between locations, from airport to hotel, from hotel to ship or wherever they need to go as part of their itinerary is called a "transfer." Each transfer is calculated as a separate cost in pricing tour packages. "You'll be transferred," brochures say in terminology that's efficient but sounds oddly like moving boxes rather than people. "Alaska Up Close will meet your flight," I wrote in my itineraries, or in other locations, "you will be picked up by_____," followed by the name of the tour operator and a contact phone number. Though I priced in all transfers required as part of itineraries, I routinely drove people other places they wanted to go without extra charge.

In addition to couples and families, I also planned itineraries for solo travelers. One of my solo travelers was booked through a travel agent in London. I met John dockside at the ferry terminal on a Tuesday two hours after midnight, after his 38-hour sail from Prince Rupert, British Columbia.

He said he drove a taxi in London, but he was quiet and not given to talking about himself. His passion was animal photography, and I wondered at the time how a taxi driver could afford such expensive vacations to photograph wildlife around the world.

It wasn't until after he returned home that I learned taxi drivers in London meet the strictest training in the world. To drive my tour van I had my vehicle inspected by a garage and local police, took a cursory medical exam and paid the city a $100 fee. He had to pass an in-depth test on London street routes and places of interest called The Knowledge, a test little changed since it was instigated in 1851. Some applicants take it up to 10 times before passing it, after preparing for nearly three years. I wished I had known that about him. Since then I've thought of him on trips to London, looking expectantly at drivers of the familiar black cabs, hoping he is well and still taking pictures of things he loves.

I arranged a trip for a Pittsburgh couple; he was an inveterate photographer, she loved to bake. When she and I both got hooked on gingersnap cookies at a trendy downtown eatery, I sent her the recipe from the restaurant cookbook along with my own counsel: "The recipe in the book bears no resemblance to our mutual addiction; use dark molasses, double the amount of ginger to see if the flavor comes close." At

Christmas I sent her a tin of my homemade gingersnaps. Marcia, if you read this, triple the ginger.

When I took photos of clients I'd send a copy back to them, and they'd often send photos they'd taken of me. I've since wished I'd taken a photo of each one. Now I'm limited mostly to the faces most indelibly etched in memory.

A couple from Minnesota celebrated their wedding anniversary in Alaska and we exchanged holiday cards for several years. She worked at Mayo Clinic; he was a teacher, and talked a local travel agency out of all their Alaska posters to decorate his classroom. She sent a newspaper clipping about Alaska from her hometown paper, as many clients did. This one was a story about the recent discovery of the remains of a hiker near an old road leading to Denali National Park, which were to be sent to Anchorage for identification. Later we would all hear much more about this hiker in a book and later a film, *Into the Wild*. She also wrote about missing the beauty and the crispness of the air in Haines, "I think the prettiest spot."

Another client, from San Francisco, sent clippings of ads for travel in Alaska, to offer ideas for advertising my own business. Clients often empathized with my on-going challenge, especially before the internet did much to bridge the gap between large and small enterprises.

In 1995 I arranged a trip for newlyweds from Bombay, the same year it officially became Mumbai. He wanted to call rather than communicate by fax, and typically called me about 7:30 a.m. my time (9 p.m. in Mumbai), after I'd left my house for my winter job downtown with the State of Alaska Permanent Fund Dividend office. After his first call I faxed back: "If you call again when I am away from the phone, please leave a telephone number where I can call you back, and a good time to reach you at your local time." I didn't want anyone to know that I worked from my house and had another job, lest they not take me seriously.

168

I'd check my home answering machine from the lobby pay phone before my work day started, then return calls as though I was making just another call from my own office. Any money I might have made planning this tour was likely spent in returning their calls. I never did the math; I didn't want to know.

The couple's June trip started in Anchorage and Denali. I met them at the Juneau airport on a Wednesday evening after they'd also cruised Glacier Bay and gone whale-watching at Point Adolphus. They brought a gift, as so many of my clients did: hand-beaded coasters, aqua with traditional black and white design.

We laughed and toured local shops together. She and I both fixed on the same sterling silver starfish earrings, but she settled on bright red bead earrings. I went back to the shop to buy the starfish for myself a few weeks later, perhaps as a reminder of the time I enjoyed with them. Both had traveled in the United States before, and seemed very much at home. Here she wore jeans; in India she usually wore saris. "They're more graceful," she said, and it was easy to picture her with black hair smoothed back and bound up, floating in brilliant red and gold silks. I planned another itinerary for the husband's aunt and uncle, also from Mumbai, and that September I met them as well.

Later came the announcement of a baby girl, born on Republic Day, January 26, 2000, a national holiday celebrating India's transition from a British Dominion to a republic.

I think of them, all four, when I read of India's booming economy and its base for U.S. technology companies. If I called for technical support on my laptop, would I speak to Mumbai? If so, it would not feel as foreign as it would have before 1995.

I also received end-of-life announcements. I started making reservations in March for a couple from Berkshire, U.K., to visit six communities, a return visit for them. We had met on their earlier trip and I looked forward to a reunion. In May the wife cancelled because of her husband's illness. In October she sent a hand-written note on a printed notice that he had passed on in September, along with her new address. "His cancer had more of a hold than we realized," she wrote, and I thought of him in his long tweed coat and neck scarf, her with gray hair bound in a bun. They were very much two as one. I see them still, caught in the time of our encounter.

When I planned itineraries for visitors I'd call them soon after their arrival, if it was in a city other than Juneau, to welcome them to Alaska and again reassure them they could call me anytime with concerns. If their trip started in my home town, I'd call them later in the tour to make sure things were still going well. And I always sent a follow-up questionnaire, welcoming them back home, asking what they told people about their trip, what they liked best and what they'd change. I enclosed a self-addressed stamped envelope and my return rate was 100 per cent.

A green ceramic bowl shaped like a large leaf sits on a table in my sun room. It was handmade by Mary, a retired educator who has since become an accomplished potter. I planned her first trip to Alaska—we met the day after the Fourth of July 1995 in Juneau, when she traveled north with two companions. We exchanged cards for a while, then lost touch. Nearly a decade later, she contacted me about a return trip to Alaska. I was no longer planning tours, but since then we've met annually for lunch in a small town midway between our rural homes in Western New York.

I sent holiday cards rather than Christmas cards, in deference to my many Jewish clients. If recipients interpreted them as Christmas cards, it was their choice. In return, people often sent hand-written letters describing their other trips, home redecorating projects, family tragedies and everyday activities like going to football games in freezing weather.

One year my holiday greeting came from nature sightings I regularly jotted on a desk calendar. That year, 1989, was a particularly poignant one and I hand-printed excerpts on a sheet of typing paper, entitling it "Seasons of the Forest–Notes from our Journal, 1989."

> January 9–a raven alights on a spruce bough, and his weight releases snow in a shimmery cascade of gentling falling stars.

> February 11–the first gaggle of Canada geese gather to feed on new green shoots in the wetlands. Spring joy on a gray winter day.

> April 12–sadness is a tangible presence among us. We can barely hear the wrenching daily reports from Prince William Sound without tears.

The *Exxon Valdez* had run aground nearly three weeks earlier, spilling some 11 million gallons of crude oil into Prince William Sound and capturing attention from far beyond Alaska. In July I was the cover person for a magazine called *Travel People*, their *Exxon Valdez* story, appearing on the cover in my red sweater, turtleneck and red skirt, wearing my button, hands resting on my spotting scope. "Judy Shuler: Nature's Partner," the cover and title proclaimed. It was unnerving to see and read about myself in the way I had written about others in my earlier life as a newspaper writer. But the reporter got it right. "It was such an emotional thing, it was weeks before I could listen to a news report or read a paper without tears," she quoted me as saying.

> April 30–the quickening. Suddenly life is everywhere. Thrush, robins, ravens, kinglets, tiny butterflies visit our yard.

> July 17–mid-morning on our favorite Douglas Island trail. Two male Sitka black-tailed deer pause in the old beaver pond, marmots run through the brush, a mother grouse corrals her chicks.

November 19–fresh overnight snow, bright winter sun, hundreds of bald eagles before us along the Chilkat River. We find tracks of a giant brown bear who came to the river to feed on spawning salmon.

"Wishing you beautiful seasons," I concluded in the best handwriting I could muster.

Some clients shared their personal family greetings. I'd planned a trip for a family of seven traveling from Memphis. That year they sent a Christmas card with a wedding photo that included the son and new daughter-in-law in their traveling party.

My Mumbai guests sent a New Year card with bright peacocks on the front a year after their return home. The personal hand-typed letter inside apologized for not writing sooner, and recounted other travels.

One of my holiday cards went to Japan, to a young woman who led tour groups. She wrote back: "Although I am traveling all over the world, I love ALASKA best. Please remember me and help me as I come back." She enclosed a small grass-green cotton handkerchief with pink and yellow butterflies in a watercolor pattern. "Maybe brings you spring flower soon. With love."

Jennifer wrote, "I can not thank you enough for making my trip to Alaska a magical one. I was overwhelmed by how much we did in a relatively short period of time. I felt as if I were a child again, awed by the spectacular beauty of Alaska. But it was the time that you spent with us that made it unique and magical."

I always hoped the warm relationships I fostered would lead to referrals for future clients. They often did, though independent travelers to Alaska were not abundant enough to exactly flood the in-box.

One of my best ambassadors was Betty, an outgoing dental hygienist. I planned her honeymoon over the snowy D.C.

winter of 1993. We phoned and faxed and phoned, and by summer she was eager for the endless planning to be over. The day following their wedding she and her new husband headed north, and we met at last. She turned out to be as engaging and enthusiastic in person as on the phone. One of the things I liked most about planning itineraries was moving through the landscape vicariously as they were outlined on paper, and traveling the state with my guests, they in real time and me in imagination. Each morning I'd review files to recall where each person was that day, and what complications might arise.

The honeymooners cut a wide swath through the state. Back home, she chatted up Alaska while she flossed and polished on her captive audience. Now each new year brings a photo card of their son and daughter with Betty's engaging smile.

Sometimes an unlikely and unexpected friendship begins with a chance meeting and an immediate empathy. Who can explain the bonds between friends any more than between lovers? The friendship between Blue and me was as unlikely as any; my friendships with other women now scattered across the country are as mysterious to me as well.

And now there was Frances.

Frances first called me in March 1995 about planning her trip north. Of all my relationships with clients, hers has been the most enduring. Already approaching 80, she was an inveterate traveler, crossing the United States by travel trailer; driving Mexico from the Yucatan; traversing Canada by rail, Vancouver to Nova Scotia; and returning to the Canadian Rockies five times. "I didn't leave this continent until I covered every road I could find," she said. Then she started looking abroad, to Europe and Australia. But like so many who called on me, she was confounded by the logistics of travel in Alaska. I met her and her traveling companion Lola, a woman a few decades her junior, at the airport late on a Saturday evening in May 1997.

Our first transport was from the airport to a downtown motel I frequently reserved. The price was reasonable, most rooms had convenient kitchenettes and the location was ideal. A major grocery store with deli counter was a half-block in one direction, the Alaska State Museum was a half-block in the other. What was then Juneau's most fashionable restaurant was just steps away. Downtown shops and cruise ship docks were an easy five to six blocks away on level ground. If guests felt like climbing downtown hills they could walk to the Alaska State Capital, the Russian Orthodox Church and blocks of colorful downtown homes. By mid-summer, flowerboxes on railings of the two upper floors dripped with hanging nasturtiums and lobelia. If I could get space there for clients, I counted it my first coup on their behalf.

We drove into the parking lot, and I pulled right in front of their ground floor room. Another score; no steps to climb.

Frances and Lola invited me into their room while they unpacked and settled in. Curious to see what was outside, Frances tugged the cord to open roll-up blinds on the kitchenette window. The roll promptly popped out of its bracket, bounced on the window sill, and crashed to the floor, striking her forehead on the way.

I looked on in horror, then relief as she began to laugh.

For a small business owner the overriding fear is not lack of customers, it's a law suit that reaches into and beyond the business to personal assets like house and home. Even with my $500,000 travel agent liability insurance, it gnawed at the consciousness. A few years earlier, my phone had rung one summer evening. A woman said she was following me on the highway when a rock struck her windshield. Could she sue? I contacted my insurance agent who said she couldn't. Thankfully the caller accepted the "no" and the matter ended.

I laughed with Frances, and promised I would go across the lot to the front desk for help in replacing the blind. As I started to walk out their door she went to the kitchenette faucet to draw a glass of drinking water. When she turned on the tap, water—hot water!—shot to the ceiling.

We laughed again, even harder. What else could go wrong?

I ran to the small check-in desk to report our plight. It was after 5 p.m., the maintenance man was gone. By now Frances was kneeling in front of the sink, looking for the shut-off valve beneath it as water splashed down into her face. It was Frances who finally stopped the flow.

Frances was tall, large-boned. In her youth I would have thought her handsome rather than pretty. I never asked personal questions of clients, though in retrospect I wish I had pried a bit more. Most people want to talk, and there was so much I never knew of the people who enriched my life beyond what they ever imagined.

I was forever seeking new out-of-the-way places to take my people, places known mostly to locals, short walks away from the crowds where they could feel Alaska up close the way those of us who lived here did. This morning I drove Frances and Lola near the end of the road on north Douglas Island. From there you could look across the water to Auke Bay and an expanse of water and mountains with little sign of human imprint. Eagles nested nearby, waterfalls glided down from mysterious origins in the forest above. On occasion a humpback whale swam by.

North Douglas was a magical place, so close to town, but so removed.

To get down to the beach, we had to step over a metal guardrail. I always watched closely when people navigated potential tripping hazards. We all stepped over with ease and started walking a gravel trail that paralleled the beach.

We looked out at the water, breathing in the day. I typically scanned a large surrounding area, ever on bear alert even though this was not as likely a place to encounter a bear as many other locations. I looked for eagles, pointed to their tree-top perches and identified their unlikely call. An eagle's call, I used to say, was "like a Tiny Tim voice in a John Wayne body." Tiny Tim was still a familiar analogy; people remembered his signature "Tiptoe Through the Tulips" song, trademark falsetto voice and his 1969 marriage to Miss Vicki on the *Tonight Show with Johnny Carson*. People would laugh at the comparison.

Like all birds, eagles drop a feather on occasion. Unlike other feathers, these are sacrosanct. Once eagles were trapped and shot for a mere 50-cent to $2 bounty on a pair of claws because the birds were viewed as competitors with salmon fishermen and fox farmers. After more than 100,000 had been slaughtered in Alaska alone between 1917 and 1952, and the fallacy of it all became clear, the eagles went from hunted to hallowed.

With Alaska statehood they came under the federal Bald Eagle Protection Act of 1940. By then they were in serious trouble in the Lower 48 states due to habitat loss, hunting and shooting, and pesticides.

I told my clients that merely possessing an eagle feather without a scientific permit or the gathering rights of a Native American for religious or ceremonial use could win them a $10,000 fine and five years in jail. I also allowed that most of us who lived here quietly had an illegal eagle feather or two. It was part of my usual patter, but rarely mattered; of all the walks I led here, we just didn't see any eagle feathers on the ground. But one day, after I gave my usual speech, we did. I repeated the law, then said that if anyone picked one up I didn't want to know about it, and I walked on ahead.

A large eagle's nest, which had blown out of the tree in a storm some years later, was close by the parking lot on North Douglas. I liked to point it out because it was so accessible, and I could set up a spotting scope in spring and early summer to look for chicks when it was in use.

There were no eagle feathers and no eagle chicks on this morning with Frances and Lola, but the magic of being here still held sway. Suddenly, without warning, Frances caught her foot, tripped and went spread eagle onto the gravel path. Once again, visions of law suits danced through my consciousness.

She brought her legs back up beneath her, raised herself up on the palms of her hands and stood up. "I'm so clumsy," she said with a laugh. A few scratches marked the place where her forehead hit and skidded on gravel, but there was no crimson river of blood as I had feared. My tension eased and we walked on, turning again to the natural world that enfolded us.

The rest of the trip was smooth: a two-night trip to Gustavus by ferry for a Glacier Bay cruise and whale-watching cruise; day cruise to Tracy Arm glacier fjord, my personal favorite day trip; the Alaska Marine Highway to Skagway for a sightseeing rail excursion on the White Pass & Yukon Route Railway; a stop-over in Haines for the Chilkat Valley nature tour and a stop at the Alaska Chilkat Bald Eagle Preserve Nature Center.

Frances was effusive in her enthusiasm for the way the itinerary had been planned.

We continued to exchange cards years after most other names dropped from my holiday card list. Although I typically guarded much of my personal life from the visitors I met, when we started summering in rural western New York, Frances and Lola were invited to visit.

Once again, Frances set out on a road trip from Memphis. We rendezvoused at a hotel about seven miles away, then I led the way to our farmhouse on Route 20, a cross-country highway that starts outside Boston and stretches 3,365 miles through 11 states and four time zones to Newport, Oregon.

Frances' health now precludes travel, but we still talk by phone and our conversations unfailingly lift me up. She always says the same thing in her rich Tennessee voice: "Child, that was the best planned trip I ever took." She sent candy from their local college; I mailed a loaf of homemade stollen. Frances continues to exclaim about our time shared in Juneau and New York. Now she has been robbed of nearly all vision but light and dark. "If anyone doubts the value of memoir, they should be in my position now," she says.

She has two regrets, she says, "I regret that I can no longer return to Italy or to Juneau."

Carol's travels here and elsewhere were in defiance of her multiple sclerosis. She came here to photograph eagles, went on to climb 11,239-foot Mt. Hood and promptly set her sights on the 14,400-foot summit of Mt. Rainier. Her letters contained photos of herself in climbing gear on western peaks, besting anything I ever thought of attaining.

In 1999 I designed an itinerary for a member of Parliament of the United Kingdom. His itinerary included numerous flights on commuter and charter aircraft, and when his scheduled trip closely followed the crash of the light aircraft piloted by John F. Kennedy Jr., he asked for aircraft type and safety records for flight services included in his itinerary. By then we were on first-name basis—in retrospect presumptuous on my part—and I pointed out the difference between an inexperienced weekend pilot and pilots with commercial licenses—also presumptuous. But I understood his concerns, and checked out the flight services I'd booked for him on the National Transportation Safety Board website.

Later I wondered why more travelers did not ask those questions. Often, it seems, we have a vacation mentality that we are surrounded by some protective bubble. How often do we cross streets without looking, walk in questionable areas and take chances we would never take at home?

Some years later I would read in *The Guardian* about his leadership role in Holocaust education. Juneau was not on his itinerary and I did not meet him. I wish I had.

There were some clients I simply wish I'd known better. I first met Dan and Sis on one of the photo tours I led to the Chilkat Valley north of Haines in November for the winter gathering of eagles. He was an avid nature photographer, but that was just one of his passions. Jazz and philosophy were others. My bookshelf holds a coffee table book he published that combines all three, *Let There Be Light, Words and Music* by Daniel Polin. The idea came, he says in his introduction, while listening to Haydn's "Creation Oratorio," then was confirmed when he discovered "Creation Jazz Suite" by Australian jazz composer David Dallwitz. He selected photos, poetry and music to relate to a particular day or event in the seven days of Creation as told in Genesis. His photos ranged from Kenya to Costa Rica to Tokyo. From Alaska he chose spawning salmon in Valdez; brown bear in Chignik; an Arctic ground squirrel and marmot near Denali. I was touched when he asked if I would write a testimonial for the book jacket, and am as proud of that as anything else I'm apt to write.

The words came easy. "Music and the natural world speak to our deepest yearnings in ways that transcend mere words." That was something I'd felt for a long time. "Like nature itself, this is a complex work that speaks on many levels and reveals itself in unexpected ways."

John and his grown daughter, Fran, arrived mid-morning by air the first Sunday in June 1996. Late that afternoon they took a flight-seeing tour of the Juneau Ice cap, after a tour of the Alaska State Museum and fish hatchery and local sightseeing. The next day they cruised Tracy Arm; the following day they boarded a small cruise ship for Admiralty Island, Sitka and Glacier Bay. There was nothing too remarkable about their itinerary, but everything was remarkable about him, including the fact he walked with crutches and one artificial leg.

I remember his enormous enthusiasm in the presence of constant pain, his spirit, the way he made you want to be in his

179

presence. His daughter was intrigued by both Alaska and Alaska men. I decided she was a natural for *AlaskaMen* magazine and sent her some issues.

Susie Carter launched *AlaskaMen* magazine where all ventures of merit start, at her kitchen table. She raised a houseful of children and foster children in California, moved to Anchorage in 1982 and opened a daycare center. But it was the single fathers needing a match that caught her attention, and she put together a magazine featuring Alaskan bachelors. The first issue came out in 1987; now she also has a web site and acts as consultant for radio and television programs.

As far as I know, Fran never moved to Alaska. Eventually she sent word of her father's passing. Slight of build, with a head of pure white hair, he remains one of the strongest images in my mind.

16. Looking Beyond Juneau

As we started booking statewide itineraries, our colleagues and outlook expanded as well. I always said "we," not "I," implying a staff, I suppose. But even in a one-person office, I knew that no one does something alone in a vacuum. "We" included my husband, who shared my life in Alaska and made it possible for me to pursue this vision. It included the other small tour operators I came to know, book on behalf of my clients and support in every way I could because I believed they could offer a close-up perspective, and I understood their struggle and their heart. It included Blue, who shared my day-to-day life with visitors and taught me about real customer service. "We" also included prior clients, who added their own insights and influence to what I did.

As I looked beyond Juneau, I thought first of the places that had captivated me as a new Alaskan. When Alaska-bound visitors asked about potential destinations I gave them my honest assessment. I didn't want any of them to come away thinking "Is that all there is?" I'd personally seen nearly every location and tour I booked, and it was easy for me to visualize the pace and flow of each day as I traveled vicariously through the itinerary I outlined.

181

First-time visitors want to see places they've heard about. I knew that usually included Denali and Glacier Bay. I looked for small operators who could fulfill my goal of showing visitors even the tourist highlights up close. Then I'd gently nudge clients to less familiar destinations and even places they might not have heard of—"the real Alaska, away from the tourist glitz," I'd assure them.

The Kenai Peninsula is Anchorage's playground. My itineraries often included a drive-it-yourself segment when travelers rented a car in Anchorage for a three- to five-day loop south of the city. I reserved overnight accommodations, and typically a wildlife viewing cruise from Resurrection Bay out of Seward. I allowed time for people to make their own discoveries at their own pace, with suggestions for things to see and do en route.

When I was a young new Alaskan living in Anchorage, I explored the Kenai with friends on many weekends, lunching in small-town cafes, digging for clams on one of the few beaches considered safe from red tide, picnicking, throwing sleeping bags on banks of the Russian River in what we later learned was prime bear country. I focused my first 35mm camera on the Kenai's varied vistas, and began a lifelong interest in photography. Our first trips were made over rough gravel roads still showing effects of the 1964 earthquake.

Seward was a favorite destination, just 125 miles and two and one-half hours of mind-bending scenery away. The Seward Highway follows Turnagain Arm, climbs through Johnson Pass and Moose Pass, then drops into Seward at the head of Resurrection Bay. It has been named a National Forest Scenic Byway, an Alaska Scenic Byway and an All-American Road, but we didn't need a declaration three decades earlier to know how special this roadway was.

But now I was living in Juneau, and I wondered if the Kenai Peninsula was as special as I remembered. It was time to revisit the Kenai and see if blind sentimentality had overtaken reality. During a break in my tours in August 1996, I flew to Anchorage, rented a car and drove the route I'd booked for clients to see for myself.

Memory had not failed me; new development did not blunt the area's charms. After my return, I wrote "If Alaska consisted of no more than the Kenai Peninsula, it would still be reason enough to travel to the 49th state."

> Rugged mountains, a 700-square-mile ice field and walk-up glacier, rolling hills covered with wildflowers, brown and black bear, perhaps 8,000 moose, rivers to fish and float, coastal fjords with tidewater glaciers, whales, puffins, coastal and inland communities with personalities as distinct as individuals. Paved highways make it all readily accessible by rental car at your own pace, though you may also travel the Kenai by air, rail or bus.

I also decided to take the Kenai Fjords National Park wildlife cruise I'd been touting as one of the state's best day trips for wildlife viewing. The commercial wildlife cruises had been just beginning as we moved away from Anchorage, and this was my first chance to experience what my clients did.

As with other destinations, I had looked for a smaller operator to give them a more close-up experience. So I set sail on the same 22-passenger vessel I booked for them. The route begins in the often-choppy waters of Resurrection Bay, and continues through a stretch of open ocean in the Gulf of Alaska. Most day trips in Alaska are on inland waters protected from ocean swells by islands that serve as barriers. In unprotected, open waters it's often not the extent of motion, but the rhythm, that catches us off guard and sends mixed signals to the body's equilibrium. In my pre-trip planning materials I cautioned clients to prepare for ocean motion by talking with their doctor about ear patches, motion sickness drugs or wrist bands, and by moving about the boat, sipping soda and eating crackers. "If you're feeling seasick, let the captain or a crew member know and get to a head or rail if you feel nauseated," I wrote.

I urged them not to bypass the tour because of fear of getting sea-sick, adding "It's nothing to be ashamed of." So did I prepare for the possibility of my own seasickness? I did not. Did I get seasick? Let's say I found an unoccupied head when I desperately needed it, and I was discrete enough that the ship's crew never knew I was sick. "Tour guides shouldn't get sick," I remember thinking after failing to heed my own advice.

"Feel rhythmic swells of the Pacific," I wrote in notes I later sent to Alaska-bound clients. If any of them got seasick, they never admitted it to me either. And the trip got positive comments on the post-trip evaluation forms.

The wildlife sightings were all I'd been saying they were: thousands of seabirds nesting on Chiswell Islands, part of the Alaska Maritime National Wildlife Refuge; tufted and horned puffins; storm petrels, oystercatchers, common murres, auklets; plus Steller sea lions, sea otters, humpback whales, orcas, mountain goats, Dall porpoises.

What stayed with me most, though, were the mountains and glaciers. The Southeast landscape seems to me like a lush embracing garden with its dense forest and meadows of wild flowers and wild berries, an inviting, nourishing place. By contrast this felt like the dawn of time itself, primordial, spare, hypnotic. In a strange way, it was terrifying and compelling at the same time.

I wanted to absorb and remember everything about it, the constant cracking of glacial ice in all directions, how you could smell the ice as well as the sea, the way the intense cold blue of the ice played against the brown of bare rock. I lived with mountains every day in Juneau, but they were like these in name only.

"This is surround sound and surround scene in one," I wrote in my notes. "Here you'll be in the midst of a 360-degree panorama, encircled by primeval rugged mountains draped with hanging glaciers like blue frosting dripping down the sides of a chocolate cake. Continually rumbling from shifting and moving, tidewater glaciers slough tons of ice before your eyes."

It was one of the few tours I regularly booked before I had experienced it myself; now I could recommend it with even more conviction.

17. Alaska Unvarnished

Closer to home, I focused on two small towns in Southeast Alaska, Haines and Wrangell. Both met my definition of authentic Alaska—unpretentious, unvarnished places where people went about their daily lives with a nod to tourism but not consumed by it. I included them whenever possible.

Visitors could travel from Juneau to Haines by small aircraft, but I nearly always booked passage by Alaska Marine Highway. The 4½-hour cruise up Lynn Canal is a cherished local getaway here, just as the Kenai Peninsula is a favorite from Anchorage. One criterion for designing my itineraries was including destinations and experiences I enjoyed as a resident and planned for our own visiting friends or family. The ferry trip was great for people-watching as well as for the unfolding wild vistas of mountains, glaciers and sea.

So often it is the stories of people that linger in our minds. On one Lynn Canal sailing toward Haines a young woman caught my eye. She looked about the same age I had been when Alaska was fresh and new to me. She wore olive hiking boots, tan cargo pants, a navy sweatshirt and black fleece jacket, requisite wear for the young in Alaska. *Frommer's Alaska* marked her as more likely a visitor than local. I sat across the aisle and slightly behind her. What I saw most was her delicate profile. What I couldn't take my eyes from was her hair, a froth of curls like Shirley Temple's three generations ago, blond with a tint of red. More than her youth, her fresh face and pale blue eyes, I envied her hair.

She sat alone, afloat in thought as much as on the sea. Was she moving up? Moving through? Had this place seized her heart as it did mine four decades earlier?

Lynn Canal is filled with stories, some far more wrenching.

Like that of every coastal community, our history includes shipwrecks. The most anguishing occurred virtually unnoticed outside the immediate area. Just as the far deadlier 1871 Peshtigo, Wisconsin, fire was eclipsed by the Chicago fire and the legend of Mrs. O'Leary's cow on the same day, the October 1918 sinking of the *Princess Sophia* was overshadowed by other world events.

World War I, a conflict that claimed maybe 14 million lives, was a few weeks from armistice. An influenza pandemic raged that would eventually kill 30 million to 50 million people worldwide (my grandmother among them). Little wonder there was scant appetite for another disaster with just 353 casualties.

When I accompanied visitors on the ferry up Lynn Canal I briefly recounted the story of the *Princess Sophia* but I didn't dwell on it. Rather, I'd point out the photogenic octagonal Eldred Rock lighthouse 30 miles south of Haines that was first lit in 1906, its construction spurred by disastrous gold rush era shipwrecks in its vicinity.

But the *Princess Sophia's* story is powerful and poignant, one worth retelling. She departed Skagway at 10:10 p.m. on October 23 into heavy rain and rough seas, typical October weather. It strayed off course and ran onto Vanderbilt Reef four hours later. Other ships came to assist as day overtook that dark night, but the captain kept the passengers on board, concerned about danger of the still rough seas and believing the storm was weakening and the ship would float free on the rising tide. He cabled headquarters for help, engineers restored power and light and heat, cooks prepared meals. But the storm retreated only briefly before wild surf and foam surrounded the stranded vessel.

Passengers wrote letters to family and loved ones while the storm raged ever stronger. The following morning, skippers standing nearby to rescue passengers estimated wind had increased to nearly 100 miles per hour and seas had risen to more than 30 feet. That afternoon the wireless operator sent a frantic distress message: "Ship foundering on reef. Come at once," but would-be rescuers were beaten back by the storm. At 5:20 p.m. the wireless operator sent another message: "For God's sake hurry, the water is coming into my room." His room was on the top deck of the ship, next to the bridge.

After nearly 40 hours with the ship wedged on the reef, bow pointing in the general direction of Juneau, the wind and waves began to pick up the stern. The *Sophia* rose, pivoted 180 degrees and slid off the reef into deep water. Rocks ripped gaping holes in the hull, tearing out virtually the entire bottom. When rescue ships could finally reach the site the following morning, only the cargo mast remained above water. There was a single survivor; an English setter owned by a passenger was found at Auke Bay, 12 miles from the wreck, starving and covered with oil two days after the sinking.

Bodies were scattered along the shores of Lynn Canal and Douglas Island, and many were recovered from beach and water over the next few weeks. Most died not of drowning, but of suffocation from the ship's fuel oil. The next year divers would recover 86 bodies floating inside the sunken ship. Vanderbilt Reef, the rocky outcropping that impaled the ship before releasing it to the depths, is now marked with a prominent lighted marker.

Alaska's continental shelf is the final resting place for more than 4,000 shipwrecks, according to the National Oceanic and Atmospheric Association. Many have historical or archaeological significance, and all have stories to tell.

In 1984, the City & Borough of Juneau commissioned former Alaska Poet Laureate Sheila Nickerson to write lyrics for choral music from her poem "Songs from the Dragon Quilt." One of the nine sections is given to the last sailing of the *Princess Sophia*. I was a member of the chorus for the world premiere concert on December 2. "Just time to say good-bye, we are foundering," a haunting refrain intoned. And if I thought about it too much during the concert, I could hardly get the words out.

Haines, just 10 nautical miles south of Skagway, was one of my favorite towns. Like Wrangell, it fell on hard times when the timber industry hit the skids. Both offered a glimpse of real Alaska. Both were gateways, Haines to the Chilkat Valley and Wrangell to the Stikine River.

18. The Council Grounds

The Chilkat Valley knits together the coastal rainforest of Southeast Alaska and the Interior landscape of the Yukon. For several years I led wildlife photographers to the banks of the Chilkat River for a gathering of bald eagles that typically reaches its apex in mid-November. Up to 3,500 bald eagles come from throughout coastal Alaska and the Pacific Northwest to feed on a late salmon run in the Chilkat River after most other rivers have started to freeze. The Chilkat is kept ice-free by warm water percolating from a huge subterranean reservoir at temperatures 10 to 20 degrees warmer than water at the surface. An alluvial fan that contains the reservoir was created 10,000 years ago as glaciers and their meltwater deposited gravel, rock and debris at the confluence of the Chilkat and two other rivers, the Tsirku and Kleheni. Each year the reservoir is replenished by enormous amounts of melted snow and ice flowing into the fan faster than it can flow out.

It was easy to capture photographic slides of eagles perching on cottonwood trees like Christmas ornaments, more than 100 birds in a single image. While it was still rainy in Juneau, fresh snow often blanketed the Alaska Chilkat Bald Eagle Preserve just 18 miles inland from Haines, making ideal conditions for observing and photographing eagles and for spotting footprints of brown bear that made their way to the riverbank in darkness.

We watched as an eagle pulled a salmon from open water, dragged it onto the bank and started to feed, holding the fish with one talon, steadying itself on the ground with the other and tearing off each bite with its beak. Another eagle would sashay along, hunched like an old man, swaying side to side, fixing its sights on the same fish. Often as not, the first eagle would yield to the interloper until still another eagle happened along and the process began anew. It's called displacement when one eagle stakes his claim to the fish, only to be driven away by another. Magpies and mergansers hovered nearby, awaiting their chance to feed.

Eagles spend a lot of time conserving energy, just sitting and perching, a boon for photographers using cameras with long lenses mounted on tripods. Sometimes they'd ride thermals, soaring ever higher over the Chilkat Mountains. It took a quick eye, fast film and a lot of skill to capture those images. More focused on my clients than on taking my own photographs, I came to appreciate the sound of the rush of air over a seven-foot span of feathers as my own indelible Chilkat Valley memory.

When I started leading tours there were no restrooms, none of the interpretive signs or boardwalks that exist today, just a couple of pull-outs for parking along the highway. Once we arrived at the eagle gathering, by 9 a.m. to capture first light, we stayed there until dusk sent us back to town around 3 p.m. The people who came with me were serious photographers. I had already warned them about rationing breakfast coffee—I wasn't about to drive back over often icy roads for a bathroom break, losing precious daylight in the process and leaving behind people at the river without a warm-up hut and access to all their gear.

I spent the week before the Chilkat Valley trip cooking and baking at home, making lemon pound cake, chocolate chip cookies and lemon bars along with stew, chili and other cold-weather dishes for lunch. I'd pack entrees from my refrigerator or freezer into the back of my van for the 4 ½-hour ferry ride to Haines, then drive from the Haines ferry terminal into town and store them in the motel refrigerator in my room. It was usually cold enough for frozen items to remain frozen if left overnight in the van. The night before serving I'd heat them in a crock pot, then transfer them into big stainless steel Thermoses just before heading out for what was called the Eagle Council Grounds. I bought cold cuts, cheese and bread from a Haines grocery store for people to make their own sandwiches. There were no snack shops nearby, and no other options until another operator began offering catered lunches a few years later. I also took Thermoses of coffee; you needed something hot just to wrap your hands around on many days.

Days were short, evenings long and activities few in mid-November. To break them up, I planned dinners in different restaurants and invited local people to come as guest speakers. I wanted people to know something of the backstory of the place they were photographing. One year I invited the mayor, who is also a jewelry maker and shop owner. Over the years Haines grew into a mecca for painters, print-makers, jewelers and sculptors in addition to the traditional Tlingit artists. I also invited Dave Olerud, whose name has become synonymous with eagles of the Chilkat Valley. At the time he was just beginning his journey of promoting eagles and the entire ecosystem of the Chilkat Valley, a journey that would take him down unimagined roads.

The State of Alaska created the 48,000-acre Alaska Chilkat Bald Eagle Preserve in 1982 to protect critical habitat for the eagles and for natural salmon runs that feed both people and eagles. It was not an easy path.

The Chilkat River would have been diverted and some of the eagles' most critical flood plain habitat would have become a disposal site for mine tailings under a proposed development of iron ore deposits in 1959. The mining consortium dropped their plan as unprofitable a year later, but the U.S. Fish & Wildlife Service sat up and took notice. The agency soon started annual counts of Chilkat eagles.

In 1972 the Alaska legislature established the Chilkat River Critical Habitat, stipulating that any use or management of the area must not harm eagle populations or habitat. It sounds innocent enough today but the move sparked major controversy as a potential threat to logging and mining. A few years later the Montana-based Aldo Leopold Wilderness Research Institute did a more in-depth study of eagle population, discovering the Chilkat bald eagle concentration was the largest known concentration anywhere throughout its range in North America. A 1977 proposal to make the critical habitat area a state park was abandoned after intense opposition from logging interests. Two years later the state entered into a contract with a local logging company that would have made virtually the entire Chilkat Valley available for large-scale clear-cut logging.

Siding with eagles was not only unpopular, it could be downright dangerous. When out-of-town biologists went to Haines for work they tended to keep their heads down. One asked her boss for a bullet-proof vest after hearing death threats in an adjacent coffee shop booth. It felt as if the entire community was polarized between logging and eagle protection.

Conservationists turned to the courts, and the National Audubon Society initiated a four-year study with the U.S. Fish & Wildlife Service. Gradually a compromise took shape that resulted in creation of the preserve and adjacent Haines State Forest Resource Management Area. Residents were guaranteed traditional use rights in the entire preserve, including hunting, fishing, trapping, berry picking and woodcutting.

Into the middle of this fray stepped Dave Olerud.

Dave, at various times teacher, mayor, chamber of commerce president and owner of a sporting goods store, was one of the Haines residents who turned their chairs around and began to see Chilkat eagles not as destroyers of the local economy, but as the basis for a new one. In 1982, the same year the Alaska Chilkat Bald Eagle Preserve was finally established, Dave founded the non-profit American Bald Eagle Foundation, which is dedicated to conservation of the American bald eagle and its habitat.

I'd read about him in the local paper, and invited him to be one of our first dinner guests on my eagle photo tours.

Dave talked about his vision for a nature center with specimens and dioramas to tell the story of the whole web of life in the Chilkat Valley, not only bald eagle but wolf, coyote, fox, mink, otter, wolverine, moose, mountain goat, deer, brown and black bear, five species of salmon, birds and more. I decided to make a donation to the center each year I took tours to Haines in the name of my business, and I invited participants to become members of the foundation as well.

By 1987 the foundation had materials to begin construction of the center at Second Avenue and Haines Highway, but no money to pay carpenters. The work itself would be done by volunteers. Walls were pre-assembled, then lifted into place. Dave was helping erect the final wall when it fell on him, crushing his back, paralyzing him from the waist down and consigning him to a wheelchair and constant pain. It cast a pale on the project and willingness of other volunteers to continue. Progress flagged, but not Dave's enthusiasm.

In 1993 he used his own savings and pensions to finish the basic structure.

When he came out of the hospital he was on 23 pills.

"People who break their back lose 10 years of life span because medication damages organs," he says, so he threw away all the pills, allowing himself an Advil every few weeks when pain is too bad. He copes by keeping his mind occupied and running television non-stop, falling asleep at 2 to 3 a.m. when he's really tired.

"I'm a problem-solver," he says. "I always find more problems in the process of solving the old ones."

His father-in-law hurt his back and lost one arm and the use of one leg in an industrial accident, Dave says. "Yet he raised three daughters with no insurance or compensation. He was also in constant pain. Now I know what he went through. The body compensates and makes you do things you never knew you could."

At the now-expanded visitor center, guests usually find Dave in his wheelchair, smiling and talking with endless enthusiasm about Mother Nature as teacher in the Chilkat Valley. When I suggested people visit the American Bald Eagle Foundation Museum, or come for the Alaska Bald Eagle Festival held every Veterans Day weekend, I'd tell them a bit about the human drama that had played out here as well.

19. He Filled a Whole Town

Blue and I first heard about Wrangell, the Stikine River, jet boat tours and Todd Harding from two Midwestern couples who booked our tours in Juneau. Prior to arriving Juneau, they had gone up the river with Todd and gotten caught on a sand bar exposed by ebb tide. Tidal fluctuations that dictate passage reach about 20 miles upriver, depending on the river's water level. The party was stranded until the incoming tide set them free several hours later. They weren't alarmed by their plight in the wilds or annoyed by the delay; they counted it as a grand adventure and a high point of their travels in Alaska.

"We need to check this out," Blue and I told each other. That September after our own business wound down we traveled to Wrangell, 11 hours by Alaska Marine Highway, to see the Stikine River with Todd. By then his passengers had transitioned from tourists to local moose hunters heading to cabins and blinds on the multi-channeled river. Cottonwood and alder leaves were turning gold, fall weather with its attendant fog and mists was settling in. Our inexperienced eyes could barely make out shadows in the early light as he steered his jet boat over sandbars at the edge of the delta, and I silently hoped he'd cancel and return to the safety of town. Todd reassured us, as he doubtless did many passengers before and after that day, and clouds lifted as we moved upriver. From estuary to endless side channels, steep cliffs, jewel-toned glaciers, countless waterfalls, snow-covered mountain peaks, the ever-changing landscape seemed to encapsulate an entire universe. I was mesmerized, and in my mind Todd and the river fused as one.

The 340-mile Stikine River is a doorway through the solid wall of the Coast Range, one of the few passages linking the coastal region of Southeast Alaska with Canada's Yukon Territory and Northern British Columbia. The river arises in the Spatsizi Plateau of northern British Columbia and flows in a large northward arc through the mountains to the west and southwest, cutting through glaciers and ragged peaks of the Coast Mountains before traversing Southeast Alaska for the last 40 miles on its journey to the sea. After venturing up the lower third of the river in 1879 and counting some 300 glaciers, John Muir pronounced it "a Yosemite 100 miles long."

The 60-mile long Grand Canyon of the Stikine, in British Columbia, has walls rising a thousand feet straight up from water's edge, at times moving so close together that they compress a 656-foot-wide river into a turbulent 6.5-foot-wide spume. Amazingly, the Grand Canyon's class V+ rapids, the highest survivable rating for a river, have been run by a handful of kayakers.

The broad, shifting, braided delta at the mouth is a world onto itself. In spring the delta is a major stopping place for great concentrations of migrating snow geese, trumpeter swan, sandhill crane and shorebirds. Hundreds of bald eagles and thousands of gulls congregate in April to feed on a run of tiny silver fish called eulachon. Deer, moose, bear and wolves call it a year-round home. Hot tubs constructed around natural hot springs are a popular destination in their own right, especially among locals. On our first trip up river our little group enjoyed our own soak, some prepared with swim suits, some au natural.

Near the river's mouth is the Garnet Ledge, mined by amateurs and professional miners for more than a century. Todd pulled his jet boat up on the beach, secured it, then led us over roots and up a fern-covered bank to a shady bluff where rough burgundy garnets, many smaller than a pea, did indeed lie on or close to the surface. Early Klondike and Stikine gold miners knew about the garnets in the 1860s. In 1892 J.D. Dana published the earliest known scientific record, "Analysis of Garnet from Wrangell."

At the dawn of the 1900s the ledge was the focus of the newly-formed all-women Alaska Garnet Mining and Manufacturing Company. Based in Minneapolis and Wrangell, the company made and marketed garnet hatpin heads, watch fobs and other jewels. But it apparently got nationwide attention not for the rough stones it mined, but for the belief it was the first corporation composed entirely of women.

I could tell the story of the women miners was a staple of Todd's narration just as I had such stories in Juneau. But it was fresh to me, and I liked the idea of these women coming north from Minnesota, just as I had done from my last job.

Wrangell garnets are not the ones you'd find smoothly polished in jewelry stores. They are too fractured for such refinement. Their charm rather lies in their rough-hewn, fresh-from-the-earth quality. For jewelers, handling such stones can be the ultimate frustration. Blue took a large garnet from Wrangell to a jeweler several years after our initial visit, asking that it be mounted into a gold setting as a surprise for me. The jeweler sliced the globe in half so it would lie flat as a pendant, surrounded it with thick swirls of gold, and vowed he would never again work with such a difficult stone. Later she gifted me with matching drop earrings. They are among my most prized possessions.

The mining company continued through 1936. Ownership eventually transferred to Fred G. Hanford, who deeded the garnet ledge to the Southeast Alaska Council of Boy Scouts of America in 1962. He left directions that land be used for scouting and the children of Wrangell be permitted to take garnets "in reasonable quantities."

Today when ferries and cruise ships dock in Wrangell, children still come to the waterfront to sell garnets they've gathered and sorted by size into muffin tins, just as many of their parents did as children. Some of the jewels-in-the-rough are still embedded in small rocks chipped from the ledge.

The Stikine River was a precursor to superhighways. Generations of Native Americans, Russian and British fur traders and gold seekers all used it for passage and coveted control. But it was more than a place of commerce; it was and is a place of spirit.

Todd once described taking a Tlingit woman and her family, along with some tourists, upriver. It was a drizzly day much like our first trip, an eerie running of the lower river through fog with visibility only a few hundred feet ahead. As fog started to lift and he was poised to speed up, she asked if she could sing to her ancestors. He held back, the woman lifted her hands and started chanting in Tlingit. Other passengers felt silent. When she stopped and brought her hands down, and other talk gradually resumed, Todd asked what she was singing. She said it was a song of thanks, a song for those who have left us and what they left us to enjoy.

The river's spell does not stop with those whose ancestors run generations deep. A young Caucasian woman from Middle America came to Wrangell by chance, made it home, and said she feels restless and unsettled when too much time passes between her trips up the river. Whether or not it was articulated, I sensed the feeling ran deep through the town. Just as Denali is simply "the mountain," the Stikine is "the river."

What is it about that river? Little known beyond the immediate area, it quietly waits for writers and artists to give it the recognition now bestowed on less worthy places.

Todd liked to push his jet boat high up into Devil's Canyon because, he said, you had to concentrate completely. It was a place where "no one's at home at 911." It made you feel totally alive. Whatever Todd was, he was totally alive. One of his former employees who traveled up the canyon with him liked to say "It was better than sex. It lasted longer and was more exciting." At times, Todd was 911. He was an EMT and volunteer fireman. And though I have limited experience and less daring in the truly wild out-of-doors, I always felt safe with him.

His younger days were the stuff of legends, and *Wild Side*, the name of his jet boat, was reportedly an apt description. I was glad I met him after he mellowed. A few years earlier he had married the woman with whom he'd lived for 18 years. A sweet, gentle girl, others described her, a foil for his blustering, full-steam-ahead personality.

Most people who contacted me about planning their Alaskan itinerary had never heard of Wrangell or the Stikine River. I tried to book as many clients as I could persuade on Todd's jet boat, housing them at the lodge owned by his brother, Bruce. I assured them that in Wrangell they would find the real Alaska, and their jet boat trips would be among their favorite Alaskan tours.

One person was 85 years old, a woman who had moved from Chicago to Los Angeles at the age of 60, newly widowed, to start a job and learn how to drive. Despite her game approach to life, she viewed the Stikine River trip with some trepidation. "It will be okay," Todd said reassuringly, promising to stop often at cabins along the river to allow her to pee. The trip was for her, as for so many others, the highlight of her Alaskan travels.

Todd always struggled. The overhead was high; there was never enough business to really pay off. Like most small tour operations, it was first of all a way to be in a place you loved.

I booked two tours with him and whenever possible I had my clients do both. One was a scenic trip up the river, the second was a trip to Anan Wildlife Observatory on Anan Creek, about 30 miles south of Wrangell. During mid-summer salmon runs, you could see black bear up close, along with an occasional more distant brown bear. At Anan, bear occasionally used the same boardwalk visitors would traverse en route to an open-sided viewing platform constructed and staffed by the U.S. Forest Service. On one visit, I looked between the platform floor boards at a black bear directly beneath my feet. Another bear sauntered by a few yards from the side railing.

Steep steps from the platform down the river bank led to a canvas-covered photo blind. Images of Anan bear are easy to recognize—black bear against moss-covered rocks, surrounded by ferns, the greens almost fluorescent against the deep shade of the river bank, with the inevitable fish in their mouth.

"Take the fastest film you feel comfortable shooting," I'd counsel my Anan-bound visitors, "and take a tripod if possible." Mountains and deep forest keep this beautiful spot in perpetual shade.

I saw Todd little more than a half-dozen times during the nine-year span I knew him. First, on my September trip up river with Blue, then on an Audubon spring migration field trip. I traveled to Anan with Todd twice, and the river twice more while accompanying clients and visiting friends. Most of our communication was by phone and fax. He would pencil in space for me on speculation, before I had firm commitment from clients and money in hand, and philosophically erase it if they cancelled.

I'd taken a few photos of him in his jet boat, none as good as I wished. There aren't many photos of him, not really good photos. He'd look into your eye, but not the camera's. He was always looking off to the side, like Martha Mitchell in that famous 1970s photo while other Washington wives all looked dutifully ahead. Was he already seeing the unseen? Did he know? I think people often do, though maybe on an unconscious level.

On a mid-July day in 2000 he returned to his boat alone after escorting a group of people up the three-quarter mile forest trail to Anan. He was later discovered lying on the wooden boardwalk, nearly back at his boat, apparently felled by a massive heart attack. No one had seen him fall. He was just 42.

Once, on a trip up river, I asked him if he wanted to have his ashes scattered on the river after he died. (My will says I am to be scattered over the ocean near Juneau's Shrine of St. Therese.) He said his family didn't want that. They wanted a place where they could come to visit his grave.

A few weeks after Todd's death, his body was cremated and his ashes scattered at Clearwater Creek where Todd had spent many hours up the Stikine.

No one who has passed, beyond my immediate family circle, has affected me as his death did. I lay rigid, eyes wide open that first night after I heard the news, unable to sleep.

"Are you all right, Todd?" I whispered to him. "Are you okay?"

Then I thought oddly that someday my own passing would be easier because he had gone ahead and broken trail. Do we look the same on the other side? I don't know, but I knew I wanted to see again that goofy, endearing, lop-sided smile, those eyes that locked on yours. He had a crusty façade, and a marshmallow heart that felt like your own private discovery if you took the time to find it.

Our relationship was nothing beyond professional and I could not explain my sense of loss to anyone, even myself. A year later nearly to the day, I went to Anan with visiting friends. A bouquet of flowers was laying along the trail where he had fallen, placed there a day earlier by his former business associate who now brought us to Anan. I took a photo of the flowers, but thought my companions would think it strange and so kept walking while I captured a blurred image.

The town is different without him, said a former employee, who had her moments of disagreement with him through the years. "I don't think people realized how different it would be."

There are people who fill an elevator with their over-the-top personality. Some people can enter a room, and you know they are there before you even see them, like smelling fresh snow on the mountaintops while clouds still hide it from full view. And then there are people who change a whole town by their presence and leave an undeniable void when they're gone.

20. How to Really Know Your Friends

To truly know someone, I've discovered through the years, travel with them, host them as houseguests or stay in their homes. These are travel adventures filled with surprises. The greatest revelations came not from people I didn't know, but from people I thought I did.

Friends from a rural area came to visit the year after I'd arranged travel for my last client. I planned their itinerary and looked forward to showing them around my home town and neighboring communities free of restrictions that bind commercial operators.

They lived in the country, how could I know she was more city than my clients from Manhattan?

Rubber boots are standard issue in our rain forest, whether with jeans or business suit. I wore them nearly every day on the streets, first red ones, then purple when I no longer dressed head-to-toe red. Even when it wasn't raining, I found them as comfortable and comforting as bedroom slippers.

When we met our friends at the airport in May I wore running shoes, but it wasn't long before we encountered someone wearing the familiar brown Xtra Tuffs.

"Look at that goober!" she exclaimed. She was incredulous when I explained they were *de rigueur*.

Listening to the things that she could not understand or that drove her to distraction re-reminded me of how life is different here. They were the very things I cherished.

We boarded a state ferry bound for Sitka, population 9,000, third largest city in our region, on a nine-hour sailing that glides among mountains and forests. Once at sea, I never want such voyages to end.

"This is the most relaxing trip we've ever had. But I couldn't live this way," she said. "It's so laid back here." Why would anyone take a ferry, she wondered, when you could get there by jet in 20 minutes?

"I'd like to take some people from a big city, where it's so crazy, and set them down here for a year," she said.

We do have quite a number of people from big cities in New York and California who come to get away from that, I told her. "But it's not for everyone."

"It would drive me crazy. I'm hyper," she said, something I was coming to realize in a way I had never imagined.

People who worked aboard the Alaska Marine Highway spoke of vacation passengers who boarded with Triple A personalities. After a day or two at sea, they'd mellow into a new disposition. It was going to take more than that for her.

I arranged a ferry trip to Haines and Skagway a few days later, and unlike all the times I'd booked it for clients, this time I would get to go along.

We'd sail from Juneau in early morning, get off in Haines for lunch with a few extra hours to visit galleries and the American Bald Eagle Foundation museum, then board another ferry for an hour sailing to Skagway, I explained. We'd overnight in Skagway, and then sail back to Juneau the following afternoon.

Everything we took to Skagway for the overnight we'd have to carry around with us in Haines, I cautioned. There was no place to stash it in Haines as we weren't spending the night.

"Take a backpack," her husband said.

"We'll have to take a suitcase then," she said. "There's no way I can get stuff for both of us in one backpack. My make-up case alone takes more room than that. It's round and fat. I have to do my face."

Maybe that's why those of us who live here are so casual, I thought. It never occurred to me to take a make-up case on our overnight trips. Well, I didn't wear that much make-up even when I was home. Most of us didn't.

"All you really need is a change of underwear," I offered, remembering many ferry trips when I had had worn the same jeans and sweater for two days.

We went to Costco and they picked out a sky blue backpack. We all pointed out ways she'd use it back home, from outings with grandchildren to going to work in their small business.

She was unconvinced. "Going to work? I don't think so."

"I learned to pack light in Alaska. The kids will never believe it."

We were traveling to Skagway to ride the White Pass & Yukon Route Railway, a favorite sightseeing excursion for many tourists and our own visiting family and friends. Shortly into the sailing from Juneau she said, "I'd like to go up to these people and ask them why they're on this ferry. My God. Four and one-half hours! Why would they do that?"

At our summer-only inn at Skagway, our rooms were on the second floor.

"You don't have any elevators?" she asked the staff in disbelief.

"There's only one in town and that's in city hall," said the cheerful young desk clerk, one of a cadre of college students working here for the summer. "We have some young strong guys to help out."

After settling into our rooms we took a walk past a field filled with RV's. She spotted one with Pennsylvania plates.

206

"Why would they come all this way to bring a camper here?" she asked. "I'm not saying it's not beautiful," she said. "There must be more."

The following morning we boarded the White Pass Railway. When I took the ride for the first time myself, I looked at the tracks ahead and high above and couldn't believe what I'd signed on for: 16-degree, cliff-hanging turns, steep grades, tunnels, bridges and trestles on the very edge of sheer granite cliffs. Even after several trips I find myself subconsciously leaning into the mountainside as the train travels narrow-gauge tracks inches from the precipice, lest I single-handedly cause the train to fall off the edge.

"Oh my God!"

How often did she say those words as the train continued its precipitous 20-mile climb from sea level to the 2,865-foot summit as the bank dropped away? "It was scary at the top," she said. But in the end the three-hour train ride was her favorite part of their trip to Alaska.

On the sailing back home we met Juneau friends who were riding the ferry to Skagway and back for the day.

"I often think about doing that but I don't get around to it," I told her. "It's a nice getaway."

Her eyebrows lifted in disbelief.

"We're easily entertained," I said. "It doesn't take much to amuse us."

"I can see that," she said, both teasing and serious. On the fishing charter we arranged for them with another friend, she said to the captain "you have to move back and forth like this for hours to fish?"

Our boat passed the Shrine of St. Therese, a picturesque stone chapel on a tiny island overlooking Lynn Canal where the loudest sounds are often from sea lions in the canal and crows who nest in spruce that completely envelope the church. About 23 miles from downtown Juneau, the Shrine is a favorite destination for fishing from the island's rocks or for simply standing at water's edge and looking out to sea. Most residents take visiting friends and relatives there for its quiet beauty.

Surveying the Shrine from the water, our friend said "why did they put it way out here?"

Well, I'd known her for years, but I barely knew her at all.

Sometimes our houseguests had such visceral reactions that it became sport to leave things lying around just to see how people would respond.

A copy of Hillary Clinton's newly published autobiography, *Living History*, sat on a bookshelf at the top of the stairs.

"Do you like her? Do you admire her?" a guest said upon noticing the book. Her voice got shriller, the question mark higher, with each sentence.

22. Running a B&D

Travelers who are looking more for a homey environment and a family setting, want to meet local people and look at their lives, they are the ones who prefer a B&B.

Only a few B&Bs had sprung up in the early 1980s in Juneau, when a thought came to mind. My husband and I always hosted family and friends who would come up from the Lower 48 for fishing and relaxation. We lived in a small cabin at the time.

I was still working for the State of Alaska Department of Corrections and several positions were eliminated and my workload grew. A change was on the horizon-the slogan was "North to Alaska." And north to Alaska they came with ships, airplanes, motor homes. No, you could not drive into Juneau. Hotels were often overbooked. The seed was planted to start a B&B. During that time my husband was still working as superintendent for a power company.

I stammered something about how she had to endure public exposure that most of us wouldn't want.

"Do you think she cared?" Shriller still. "She had affairs too."

"I didn't know that," I said.

"Of course not as many as Biiilllll. She's about my least favorite female on this planet."

"She's power-hungry," our houseguest continued.

"I think that's sexist," I said. "Men are ambitious, women are power-hungry."

"Men can be power-hungry too," she said back.

"Well, I think it's applied more to women."

"I guess you don't think she's as bad as I do."

"I guess not."

Since I already operated my tour business, which also started as an idea, B&B just followed that path. Both are people businesses.

Around that time JR retired and we spent winters in Arizona, came back in April/May. JR devoted his time to sport fishing with family and friends who would come up from the Lower 48.

Every year when we returned from Arizona we looked for a house to lease with option to buy. Since I never knew what location this would be, I could not do any advertising for my B&B.

"What am I going to do with my friends when they come?" JR wanted to know.

"You could line them up in the garage," I told him. "You could get some cots and sleeping bags."

That's what he did. Now come breakfast time, come these scraggly guys out of the garage, needed a shave and a shower but of course they couldn't use the shower because my guests were using the shower. But all sat around, had some breakfast, had a good time, everybody did what they were going to do. I was busy shopping for towels, wash cloths, bedding, soap, cleaning and laundry supplies (you need a lot of that). The kitchen had to be stocked. Altogether we had three bedrooms. We used two of them for guests and we had one.

I was ready for my guests. I also drove tours at the same time and could not always be there for breakfast. My dear friend Doreen offered to bake bread, cook breakfast and serve and clean up while I was busy with tours. I was also still working part-time for the state but had flexible hours so I could run home during lunch break, put bedding in the washing machine, clean up, getting ready for my next guests.

That first summer it was word of mouth advertising. Sometimes my co-workers wanted to know if I was coming into work that day, and another would say "No, I don't think so, I just saw her van driving by. She's doing tours."

Sometimes Red would bring her birding group over for breakfast after birding so we kept the money in the family, so to speak.

It was more than a bed and breakfast, it was a B&D I called it. That was breakfast and dinner because Jerry would go out fishing and come evening when he had a couple of salmon or whatever he had, he'd say "How about you guys staying for dinner? I'm putting the salmon on the grill." Of course nobody said no.

One couple, two engineers from Las Vegas, decided to get married at the glacier while they stayed with us. The wedding clothes were hiking clothes and the location was the glacier.

We took our groups usually to a salmon bake that was not too commercialized. It was down by Thane Road where you could see the cruise ships come and go. This friend of ours, George, he had also a museum there. The dining room looked just like it did during the mining days. He had beautiful halibut, he had salmon and it was always a great feast and it was really fun to be down there. You could go outdoors. It was called the Ore House. Today it's run by his son and his wife. Of course some people made fun of it and said let's go to the Whore House.

The wedding was all a hurried deal. I helped get the cake together; I bought it in a grocery store. We had at the same time also a German group in so it was a great big party, everyone met each other.

We took photos for them in our living room in their hiking outfits

Another year when we returned from Arizona we found another house to lease, at the foot of Thunder Mountain. We got this place ready, just like we did the other house the year before. In a few days we were ready for guests.

One morning when I asked how everyone slept, one said "Okay, but I heard water running all night." I had no idea where the water originated. I knew I didn't have a faucet running and I checked the bathrooms. After they left I opened the closet door in their bedroom and heard water rushing through as well. JR and I investigated and we had water running under the house like a river. It originated from snow melt on Thunder Mountain. We got a sump-pump and it was working overtime, but we got everything ready for our next guests. I told JR, "You don't have to go out fishing any more, you can do it right here in the closet." It was a story good for laughs.

Red came over one day after a tour and watched me watering a plant that she had brought over. She said, "What are you doing?" I said, "I'm watering that plant, I don't want it to die." Oh that one, she said. "It's artificial."

We had a good laugh especially since I had studied biology the year before in the fall, and when we did field trips all the plants were half dead. I thought it was a plant I hadn't met yet.

A B&B is a lot of work, a lot of planning, but also a lot of fun. You will meet some very interesting people. Some will ask about the history of where you live, even if they already know all about it. They just want to know whether you know it. That's when you can bombard them with the local flavor, stuff you won't find in a book. I keep thinking about it, and another book is forming in my head. "Juicy Juneau," I may call it. You'll hear different languages, but it's amazing how music and dance can bring everyone closer together. We had a lot of fun, a lot of laughs, which resulted in repeat business and clients became friends.

If you like people business it's a great way to go. Remember, I did this without permanent location, cell

---

Our New York vacation home often felt like it was located in a bastion of conservatism, but it was no more so, I learned, than within our own close circle. Who knew?

Most of my clients were independent travelers on their own, but I did work with a few groups assembled by tour operators, mostly from London where I was represented by Glynn, a promoter of nature tours around the world. One small group arrived by cruise ship, then extended their stay in Southeast Alaska. They overnighted at the B&B that Blue ran in addition to her tours, took a two-day trip to Glacier Bay, cruised to Haines, took Todd's jet boat trip up the Stikine, and went flight-seeing over Misty Fjords near Ketchikan. As always, I followed up with a critique form. Were your guides good? Were the accommodations clean and comfortable? Was the pace too

phone or computer. If I can do it, anyone can. Find a location that's in a good area. You need to check on zoning, and whether your neighbors object, for there will be more cars. You have to provide parking space. Find a name for your business, get a business license and insurance, which is very important. You can join a B&B association. As a member you will pay a fee, but they will also screen your clients for you, and they will inspect your place for cleanliness and safety. They will also give you hints.

In 2011 I visited Juneau and Petersburg again, and visited good friends that I had helped getting their B&B organized. They had asked me what would I think of this and that. The husband is now retired from commercial fishing, and his wife, from teaching school. You will get a Norwegian breakfast there that one can only dream of. They have repeat business from Germany; their clients leave fishing gear stored there, and come back for halibut fishing every year.

---

fast? Too slow? What did you like best about this trip to Alaska? What did you like least (not counting rain)? What would you change?

The question about the least-favorite aspect brought a response new for me.

"Her (referring to a member of the group) unjustified complaining about non-existent or trivial hiccups. Requiring someone to share a room with someone as her is perhaps rather unkind." She may have been surprised by the effect she had on her fellow travelers. In her own letter to me some months later she wrote "I loved, I love Alaska. I have traveled a lot, my wish being to know as much of our planet before I die: nature, civilizations, history, geology, art which is the most beautiful accomplishment of men-on-earth. Alaska is unique.

And I am sorry not to have been able to go and see more." I'm sorry her companions did not see this side of her.

Two couples cruising with another woman in 2000 likely didn't know her too well either, according to an account in the local newspaper. The solo woman reportedly clashed with her long-time friend over appropriate dress for Friday dinner aboard ship. She planned to wear a black velvet skirt and top; her friend strongly disapproved of her choice.

As the ship sailed from Juneau and approached Ketchikan the following morning, someone discovered the woman's bed had not been slept in the previous night. Her belongings were still in her room. Concerned she might have fallen overboard, cruise ship officials contacted the U.S. Coast Guard. A search ensued, retracing the 225-mile path of the cruise ship between the two cities.

Alaska State Troopers subsequently located the missing woman at her home in Michigan. Without telling the crew or her companions, she had ended her cruise in Juneau and booked a flight home, carrying only her purse. She felt like a fashion victim, the 73-year-old passenger told police.

The Coast Guard probably felt like a victim too. A few days later the *Juneau Empire* reported they spent $63,541.20 in the search: 7.3 hours' use of a 47-foot Coast Guard boat at $10,884.30; 2.2 hours' use of a second 47-foot boat at $3,280.20; 5.8 hours' use of a Jayhawk helicopter at $45,559; several hours' use of a watch stander who made urgent radio broadcasts, $420; and 6.1 hours' use of a 25-foot boat, $3,397.70. Troopers also threw in four hours of time.

Ship computers track movements of passengers and crew with an ID card they show upon boarding and leaving the ship, but apparently recorded no evidence she left the ship in Juneau.

Blue lived in Denver before she moved to Alaska three decades ago, and when she returned there as a widow to be closer to family, Kathy and I flew south for a visit. I knew each of them better than they knew each other. Blue, so organized and methodical, Kathy, who likes to say if you want to make God laugh, make plans. The surprises lay in what they would learn about each other.

"What time is it?" Kathy asked early on in our trip.

"We have to chip in and buy you a watch," said ever-punctual Blue who'd crafted a daily itinerary for our visit with as much precision as we used to do for tourists to Alaska.

"I have some watches at home," Kathy said. "Some work, some don't. I usually don't care much what time it is."

One evening Blue planned to make a Denver omelet for supper, and picked out three peppers, green, yellow and red, at a large discount store. The sign said two for a dollar, 50 cents apiece. She took them to a check-out station staffed by a wizened man, maybe late-70s, who moved like a film running at the wrong speed. He held up one pepper; it rang up at $1.59. When Blue protested, he demonstrated with each pepper, slowly, deliberately, and seemingly with a touch of self-satisfaction when each priced out the same. We left the store without them.

Later Blue mentioned the check-out man to her daughter, who was personnel manager at the store.

"Mom, we know he's slow but he's such a nice man and he means well."

"Yes, that would be Blue's daughter," I thought to myself.

When a day of shopping did us in, the menu changed from home-cooked to Mexican food at her local hangout.

"Don't get too settled," said the always-organized Blue when we reached her home. "Let's go out before we're tired," as if we weren't already.

"I'd enjoy it more if I could sit and relax for half an hour," said Kathy, who always had a book at hand.

"Okay," Blue said. "But no reading."

"Okay," Kathy agreed.

When she napped and read on Blue's living room sofa, Kathy sank so deeply into the cushions we often could not tell whether she was there.

"I am one with the sofa," she proclaimed.

Blue and I headed for her screened-in patio to watch the afternoon's last sun. Kathy went into the bathroom, and when she returned after a long absence I asked if she was okay.

"I'm fine," she told me out of Blue's hearing. "I went in there and I started to read."

The highlight of our visit was to be an overnight stay at the hot springs at Glenwood Springs. She booked passage on Amtrak's *California Zephyr*. We left her home by cab shortly after 6 a.m., to the sounds of Nigerian music.

Our departure, on Train No. 5, was scheduled for 8:30 a.m. and we wanted to allow plenty of time. We'd have all the time we needed and more. Train No.5 got caught behind another train that was broken down. Ours should arrive by 10 a.m., we were assured at the downtown depot.

From our shopping trip the day before we already knew that just out the door, a block to the right, then across the street, was the Tattered Cover book store. Kathy and I both honed in on it, not only because of our affinity for independent book stores but because we loved the name. Cell phone in hand, I called to see when they would open. It was 9:10 a.m. and they were already open. Blue, who clearly disapproved of our side trip, agreed to wait at the station and watch our luggage while we took another spin through the old and thoroughly engrossing store. We promised to be back before 10 a.m.

We had barely checked out their bakery counter when a staff member approached and asked if I was Judy Shuler. It was unnerving to be called by full name by a stranger in a strange city. He had a message: we were to return to the train station right away. I fretted about how Blue had described me that I was so readily recognized.

216

"I told him you had a red purse," she said.

We walked in sheepishly under Blue's stern eye, grabbed our bags and headed for the end of the line to exchange tickets for a boarding pass. The ticket agent said we'd need ID and I pulled out my Alaska driver's license. Kathy went through the motions of searching for hers, but already knew it was in the brightly embroidered pouch she wears for travel, and she'd left it back at Blue's home an hour away. Blue showed thinly veiled exasperation; I tried to control my own dismay.

"I'll go back to the house and wait for you," she said when we considered the likely outcome of trying to board without ID.

We approached the station agent like children in a classroom trying to avoid notice by the teacher. Blue had purchased the tickets in her name. He asked to see her ID, and exchanged all the tickets for boarding passes. We gratefully proceeded to board.

Though our vacation plans were saved, we noted how easy it was to get aboard public transportation even after 9/11, how lax security truly was.

When we returned to the Denver depot after our overnight outing, Kathy and I headed for the restroom while Blue lost us again as she headed straight out the door.

Blue and I are an easy fit after our shared years in tourism.

"I'd travel with you again," Kathy told me as our trip came to a close. Whether she and Blue would find common ground as traveling companions was a question for another day.

21. "Alaska As I Imagined It Would Be"

It is no longer possible to do what Blue and I did. Buy a van. Get a sales permit and insurance. Treat tourists as you would a visiting aunt.

Perhaps it never was. The economy of scale simply wasn't there. We all fantasized about having our tours sold aboard cruise ships in those early years, even while knowing we couldn't offer the sales volume to make it financially worth their while. Yet there were many others who dreamed as we did, who came to the streets of downtown Juneau to share something about which they felt passionate, and hopefully make some money at the same time.

Most taxi drivers were just starting to catch onto the idea of being tour guides. In the beginning I directed people in search of a cab to pay phones across the street from Marine Park because there were none to be seen.

There were guided horseback riding tours near glaciers, small power scooters and ricochet rides in town, walking tours, motor tours in everything from camouflage-painted jeep to classic car to van to limousine. Each brought their own spin.

When cruise ship passengers approached one of our counterparts and asked about her tour, she said, "I'll take you to the corners." She went on to explain that she meant the little out-of-the-way places where buses couldn't maneuver and most others wouldn't think to go. Cope Park, a small park on the lower reaches of Gold Creek, was one of her favorite destinations and one that I sometimes included as well. Right in town, just downhill from the Governor's Mansion, you could lose yourself in the froth of the stream that started as snow melt in mountains behind the city and yielded the first gold nuggets that birthed this city.

Each of us, the handful who brought our assorted vehicles to the docks in the mid-1980s, had our own corners, and we fanned out through greater Juneau on tours of our own creation.

My corners varied with the season and who was on board.

Before pulling my van away from the curb I'd feel out the interests of my passengers, then alter my route to accommodate them, something I knew the big bus companies could not do. I routinely asked if people were on a tight schedule. Most times they were happy for a leisurely pace that allowed for unscheduled stops, but always with the caveat we return in time for their assigned sitting at the next meal.

If I had builders on board, I might drive them past a new housing development. Everyone was interested in the cost of houses and lots. I regularly read the classified and display ads to keep up to date. I knew which hillside streets offered the best views; I found a vacant hillside lot across the channel on Douglas Island where everyone could fantasize about their dream home overlooking city and harbor below.

I pressed biologists I knew through our local Audubon chapter for locations of the most visible eagle nests. One nest was unusually low and on a gravel residential road for all intents and purposes a dead end. By late May, when eggs typically hatched, I'd start watching for activity at the nest. Even before a chick was visible, we could watch parents alternate tending

23. Bridging Language

When the big tour operators had a bus full of German tourists, they hired me to narrate the tour in German. On occasion I also gave safety instructions for helicopter glacier-landing tours.

I gave the same tour as I did for passengers in my van—the bus drivers were always glad they didn't have to do it. Applause and tips were great, especially when I had one of my favorite drivers, Ed. We would split tips and we each ended up with around $50 for the tour, plus our pay.

One thing about Germans—they were always on time. I missed a tour once when the electricity had gone out at night and my alarm clock didn't go off. We used taxis to get them to their destination. That bill—ouch!

Not all translations were related to tour buses. Once I was asked by the Alaska State Troopers to help them with a case in Gustavus (near Glacier Bay). Two German friends had camped on the beach overnight.

---

the nest and bringing food to the chicks. I'd set up my tripod and spotting scope some distance down the road to offer close-up views without invading the eagles' comfort zone.

No one was more excited than I was about every bird we saw, every animal sighting. I treasured the out-of-the-way stops even more than my passengers did, even if a particular one only came around once every few weeks or once a summer.

Most people seemed unfamiliar with nature guidebooks. I'd pull one out if I wasn't sure about identifying a bird or plant, or simply to show them an illustration. Sometimes I'd say, directly or indirectly, that I hoped tuning into nature here would help them to see it with fresh eyes back home. My go-to author was

In the morning, only one was there. The remaining traveler said he had no idea where his friend had gone—his money belt and wallet were left behind. Troopers had asked me to identify the contents to notify his family.

About two months later, I heard a knock on the door. I could not see the face of the person who knocked—it was hidden by the huge bouquet of flowers she held. It was the mother of the young man, wanting to thank me for helping. At that time she did not know anything further, but she suspected that her boy had gone into Canada. She told me he had cleaned out and stripped his room in Germany before he left home, and that he had always wanted to wander out into Canada.

Some day I mean to ask the Troopers if he has surfaced, or if they know anything about him, if the case is still open. After 30 years, I still think about him.

Bob Armstrong, a friend from Audubon. A retired fisheries biologist, he turned his passion for birds and outdoor photography into a whole library of guidebooks and newspaper columns I regularly clipped for reference. Whenever I could book a small group interested in birding I would try to schedule him as guide. I hoped they'd realize what a gift it was.

I felt as if I was the conductor, the stage director. The symphony and the drama were already here. The score was the music of this wild place. All I had to do was lift the baton, open the curtain, and take a bow at the end.

Blue and I shared an interest in photography and were ever searching for new photo spots for our passengers. When we began taking people into the meadow at Brotherhood Bridge to photograph wild flowers close up, we'd have the place to ourselves. We knew exactly where to find clumps of wild iris in early June, just below the bank, before the meadow was filled with the showier succession of lupine and wild celery. The much-photographed fuchsia fireweed followed in mid-June and July. Wondering what I could do on a photo tour if a day was particularly rainy, I set out on my own on just such a day, and captured close-ups of iris with raindrops that are among my favorites to this day. When Blue and I drove up Blueberry Hill residential streets to share their stunning view of harbor and cruise ships below, we'd be the only ones other than local residents.

We all watched each other, of course. We'd look through each other's windows to see how many passengers our competitors got, and mentally calculate their take of the day as well as our own. We'd copy ideas from each other. When taxis and even occasional buses began adding Blueberry Hill to their route, residents took note of the growing string of traffic on their quiet streets. They were not pleased with what they saw. It was the beginning of the erosion of our ability to travel our hometown freely with passengers. As tourism got bigger and bigger and local people sensed their favorite hiking trails were being overrun with commercial operators at their expense, the benign innocence began to slip away.

My file still holds a yellowed letter I punched out on a manual Olympia typewriter, dated April 16, 1984, asking the U.S. Forest Service for permission to take visitors on a quiet unimproved trail on North Douglas Island. But the land in question actually belonged to the City and Borough of Juneau.

When I contacted the proper landowner, they'd never been asked a question like that before. They didn't see any reason it wouldn't be all right and I was granted permission. No formal permit, no fees were involved.

The trail wasn't well-known beyond local residents, who counted it their personal jewel. The parking pull-out near the trailhead had room for only a couple of vehicles, and my van was highly visible. I'd lead people down a small but steep bank, and soon we'd be inside deep woods. One of our local naturalists coined the name "cathedral trees" for the behemoth, centuries-old Sitka spruce that have escaped loggers' saws. These weren't that old or large, but it nonetheless it felt to me like a holy place. It was mossy and cool, filled with ferns. I'd point out the nurse logs, tall trees that fell with so much moisture inside they provided a base not only for new shoots with their own DNA, but for a host of unrelated small ferns, moss and lichens. We'd smell the forest infused with dew.

I called the Sitka spruce the original integrated multi-story housing. In the penthouse, bald eagle and raven claimed observation platforms, along with Northwestern crow and Steller's jay, squawky, aggressive, and smart beyond reason. I'd often quote Henry Ward Beecher's sentiments: if people were birds, very few of us would be clever enough to be crows.

A little below the top, eagles build nests bigger than a king-size mattress.

Blue grouse roost in lower branches. In April you can hear the deep hooting of grouse throughout the forest as males curry the favor of a mate. A male creates the sound by inflating air sacs on either side of his neck. The patches of bare skin covering the air sacs are discretely warmed and camouflaged by feathers when he doesn't need them to make a suitable impression. For sheer exhibitionism, strutting and willingness to be a fool for love, the world of birds is the place to look. Though most visitors are too late to witness the mesmerizing antics of avian courtship, we'd often see mama grouse leading her brood along the road in August.

Most people noticed the graying strands of lichens that we call Old Man's Beard. "In some places it's so thick that one acre of timber might contain nearly one and one-half tons in dry weight," I'd say, And no, they don't seem to hurt the trees. And yes, they feel scratchy like an old man's beard. When winter storms tear clumps of lichen from the trees and scatter them over the forest floor, they become available to deer for food.

We'd watch antics of the forest's sauciest resident, the red squirrel, mere ounces of non-stop vigilance and energy. Weighing as much as three sticks of butter, the squirrels can stretch to about a foot long, nearly half of that in bushy tail. I'd point out their huge caches of "empties," spruce cone cores that squirrels had cleaned of their seeds.

In winter, spruce and hemlock boughs create a canopy that holds snow from the forest floor, providing shelter for Sitka black-tailed deer and access to small forest plants for food. Porcupines feed on the inner bark of spruce. Hollows around the roots provide day beds for brown and black bears.

In spring the new chartreuse tips of spruce boughs can be harvested to make spruce tip jelly and even a beverage. A garden column in 1984 gave directions for the beverage:

> Cover a peck of spruce tips with boiling water, let it cook, then drain the liquid into a large bowl. Add two pounds of sugar and 1/8 teaspoon yeast and stir well. Bottle immediately. Prepare for an exploding bottle or two if the tips weren't tiny and new.

It was so much nature to cover in a single tree.

We'd cross a small wooden boardwalk spanning a stream filled with skunk cabbage, their leaves still showy though the early flowers had long since fallen away. On our left was a large long-abandoned beaver pond, which one morning reflected two Sitka black-tailed deer in perfect stillness on the shore.

On we walked, from forest to muskeg.

"Some of these trees could be a couple hundred years old," I'd say, pointing to what looked like foot-tall bonsai. "The water table is so high that it stunts their growth. Their roots are drowning." The shore pine that survive here may grow only five to 15 feet high and less than 10 inches around in 300 years.

Muskeg is wet, acidic and too spongy to step in from the boardwalk. If anyone set a foot lightly on the ground to test my words, they quickly pulled it back from the ooze. Dead plants that fall on dry land soon rot, thanks to bacteria and fungi that break them down. But plants that land on water or supersaturated soil are sealed off from air, and they decay slowly. Muskeg is an accumulation of dead plants in various stages of decomposing. Sphagnum moss lies near the surface, the same type of moss sold in garden centers to loosen flowerbeds and retain moisture. Here it keeps water from draining through the soil, so absorbent it can hold up to 30 times its own weight in water. The whole system is nourished by our cool summers and abundant rainfall.

It was not a place that inspired lingering, with its foreboding air of slow death. We continued on, back through the forest, down a steep bank and onto a rocky beach. When I first brought people to this trail, we held onto tree roots to steady our way up and down the bank, a formidable feat for those with bad hips or knees or challenged vision. Trail Mix, a volunteer group then numbering fewer members than fingers on your left hand, was quietly maintaining and improving miles of trails throughout greater Juneau. Mary Lou, a prime mover of the group and another good friend through Audubon, shortly oversaw construction of wooden steps with railing to help negotiate the bank.

"They're your steps, you know," says her husband Jim more than 25 years later.

"I know," I respond. If we are lucky, we know a handful of people in our lives that we so admire that we are in awe that they count us as friends. Mary Lou and Jim King are two of those.

The total distance from van to beach was about three-quarters of a mile. But what a collage of habitats condensed in such short distance. Southeast is like that. Ocean to beach to mountain, wetland to forest in less than the length of Central Park.

From the beach I'd point to a small island, Shaman Island, named for stories of Tlingit shamans buried within. At the lowest tides, a couple of times a year, the sea surrenders a small isthmus of land allowing foot passage from beach to island. A minus-four-foot tide is best, when there's a window of about two hours to make the round trip without getting stranded. Along the way red and green starfish drape over the rocks and anemones half buried in the sand squirt tell-tale plumes of seawater into the air.

The timing was too tight and too critical to even think of taking visitors all the way; it would be a venture left to the locals and their intrepid house guests. Instead we would explore tide pools when the tide was out, looking for tiny crab and sea urchins. I'd point out purple mussels firmly attached to rocks.

"They anchor themselves by spinning fine threads called byssus threads," I'd say, gently pulling on a mussel to show how tightly it was attached.

The beach was also a good place to see eagles calling from tree tops at water's edge, their favored look-out for spotting the salmon that make up so much of their diet. Some people were visibly disappointed when we walked out far enough to look to our left and see a small house constructed near the beach. It was a reminder that though we felt a world away, we hadn't strayed that far from development.

Locals would smile and nod when they saw me and my little groups. This was still the era of benevolence toward tourism. It was fun to see out-of-towners. They were looking at the things we loved and took such pride in. When the State of Alaska unveiled generic promotional ads for television at Alaska

Visitor Association conventions, local representatives of major cruise and tour lines teared up at the beauty and mystique of the Alaska they portrayed. Many felt a catch in their throat when the Alaska Flag Song was sung.

Sitting on a big log in a pause on our walk to Outer Point, one young man said "This is Alaska as I imagined it would be."

22. Wal-Mart Moves In

Nine years after I started taking visitors to the Outer Point Trail, a tour operator with wider aspirations than mine also cast an interested eye on this gem of a trail. A guiding company applied for a permit to take groups of 10 to 12 people on nature walks along the trail four times a day. It was a watershed moment, the end of innocence.

Locals weren't smiling any more. "Their trail" was being sold, and they felt they were being sold out.

After some painful meetings and a flurry of letters to the editor, peace of sorts was achieved, and eventually a new trail was constructed nearby to separate commercial groups and locals. More public trails were subsequently opened to commercial guides, all by permit and with a user fee only feasible if you were dealing in volume cruise ships delivered.

As tradeoff, some trails were designated strictly off-limits to any commercial operator. When lupine bloomed at Brotherhood Park I could no longer take people to the sites I'd so carefully observed and noted on my calendar for years. A few times I parked nearby, told people where to walk on their own, and explained I could not accompany them. And I'd look around nervously hoping no one would see and report me. For someone who wanted to do everything above board, it was no way to run a business. Soon I could not offer anything different from the big bus tours.

Personal service was the antithesis of volume but it was growing apparent that without volume we could not survive.

Street congestion grew in the small downtown area constrained between mountain and sea. More and bigger ships meant more float planes taxied up to cruise ships for flight seeing tours; more helicopters flew down channel en route to glacier landings and walkabouts.

When Blue and I first drove to mountainside residential streets for views of the city and ships below, we noted how the sounds of moving cars and barking dogs bounced between the mountains with clarity that belied their distance. Those same mountains now amplified the sounds of aircraft beyond the levels of acceptability. Once again, people were alarmed by the changes around them.

There was a growing realization that tourism was big business. But cruise ship tourism was still seen as a "clean business," unlike natural resource extraction industries like gold mining, oil drilling or timber harvest. Now another truth was about to set in. The equivalent of a small town, a couple of thousand pampered customers and half as many crew account for lots of individual showering and flushing, to say nothing of commercial kitchens and photo darkrooms, spas, hair salons, clinics and about anything else in your average town. Where did we think all that waste was going?

Well, we didn't think about it.

Cruise ships have called here for longer than most people would imagine, following the same route used for centuries by salmon, whales and indigenous people. In the late 1800s and early 1900s, passenger steamships were already the place to be, albeit without the amenities or environmental sensibilities of today's cruise ships. With no indoor plumbing and no holding tanks on board, passengers put chamber pots outside their cabins for emptying over the railing in the morning.

The first thing locals noticed as ships came in ever-increasing numbers was the smoke emission. The state employed an inspector to go dockside, look up through the smoke plume and gauge the opacity. If the smoke was light gray and easy to see through, it was given a good grade. Dense smoke was written up and reported, a basis for contacting the ship's personnel to urge improved boiler efficiency.

Later, concerned citizens would learn they should have been looking down instead of up.

One of the world's largest cruise lines was indicted in 1998 for lying to the Coast Guard after one of its ships was photographed dumping oil while it returned to home port in Miami five years earlier. They were not only dumping, they had a bypass pipe to circumvent the system designed to separate oil, and a set of false books kept for the Coast Guard.

Juneau and the State of Alaska took note. That same cruise line was regularly plying the waters of Southeast Alaska. The state filed its own suit after the cruise line admitted to dumping toxic materials and oily bilge in Southeast waters in the mid-1990s, including dumping dry cleaning chemicals into Gastineau Channel in front of downtown Juneau. Once toxic wastes from gold mines were likely dumped into these same waters, but we tend to take a different view of such things today.

The Alaska Department of Environmental Conservation went into high gear looking at wastewater handling, air emissions and oil spill response. What they found shocked them. Systems designed to treat black water or toilet waste were failing to meet federal standards 75 percent of the time. Unregulated gray water (water from sinks and showers) also tested with high levels of fecal coliform where there should have been none at all. And all that was being dumped directly into the ocean, as close as three miles from land. When the results came out, the governor stood in Marine Park, a cruise ship docked behind him, and proclaimed the cruise industry would not operate in Alaska waters without cleaning up its act. It was another watershed not only in local relationships with the cruise ship industry, but for the industry worldwide.

Locals felt as if their home town was spinning out of control. They were angry at pollution and at their own naivety in not recognizing tourism as an industry like any other, capable of damaging the environment as much as oil drilling, but operating with no oversight.

After meetings, hearings and studies about the minutia of waste products, state regulations went into effect for sampling all waste to be discharged into marine waters and recording where and when and how much was discharged. The public was not entirely mollified. In 2006 Alaska voters passed a Cruise Ship Ballot Initiative mandating an Ocean Ranger program in which marine engineers licensed by the U.S. Coast Guard ride cruise ships operating in Alaska to monitor compliance with state and federal environmental law.

In the mid-1980s we could look at tourists walking down the street and match them up with which ship they arrived on. We had the polyester cruisers, budget travelers without much money to spend in town. We had leather pant/fur jacket cruisers from teak-lined luxury liners that were a boon for the fine art galleries and upscale jewelers.

Cruise ship capacity has increased eight-fold since Blue and I hit the streets, and it has become the travel of choice for those on a budget.

But local attitudes toward the industry that dominates coastal Alaskan summers is mixed.

A local resident who normally summers out of town went to the Juneau dock on a rainy morning, umbrella in hand, to meet people she knew. But she missed them in the crowds and instead filled her time people-watching. "They pour out and it's never ending," she says incredulously.

A friend who lives in a downtown condo removed from cruise ship congestion recently took her first cruise, to the Bahamas. She had to give a credit card number, her first exposure to the onboard "cashless society" that can render passengers speechless when shore excursions, beverages, tips, other extras are tallied at cruise end. Passengers were gathered into a large warehouse and divided into groups for boarding.

"We were told we couldn't board yet because the previous cruise hadn't vacated."

"I felt like I was being led to the gas chamber," she joked to her Jewish traveling companion. "I said it because I knew she'd take it the right way," said the lifelong Alaskan, whose politics and outlook make her among the most inclusive of people.

The resident of a Douglas Island waterfront condo, with windows high enough to hold mountains and sky above the cruise ship docks, counts return of the first ship in the spring as the brightest day of the year. He loves the behemoth ships that fill his windows, how they sometimes arrive enshrouded in fog until morning sun releases them from the mists.

Such are the divided opinions as cruising continues its popularity with travelers through good times and bad.

Tourism is as seasonal as farming, of course—and just as subject to the vagaries of weather, consumer preference, events and circumstances far beyond the control of entrepreneurs both large and small.

The total number of tourists in Alaska has changed since Blue and I began meeting them, but so has the way they come. In 1984 the total number of visitors was estimated at 800,000 with just 125,000 coming by cruise ship. By 2007 the total number coming to Alaska for vacation had more than doubled to 1.7 million, but the number coming by cruise ship was nearly a million, or considerably over half.

Well before my first day on the dock I talked with a lot of people about my plans. My first stop was the now-defunct Alaska Division of Tourism. Their mission was promotion of independent travel, the kind that leaves the most money behind in the state. Public funds were committed to generic advertisements and brochures in a public-private partnership that was the envy of the nation. In 1985 Alaska ranked seventh in public sector tourism funding among the 50 states. Within six years it had dropped to 27th place. In 2005–2006 it ranked an estimated 38th.

Nine of the 10 top states in terms of total tourism marketing budgets get 100 percent of their budgets from the public sector. Here 50 percent of the funding now comes from public funds. The balance comes from the industry itself, where the biggest players are cruise ship companies with land-based components. Who could be surprised if people think the only way they can see Alaska is from the sixth deck cabin and 40-passenger bus, or "motor coach," as the operators prefer to call them? Even 15 years ago people told me they wanted to come on their own, but had no clue how to do it except by cruise ship.

Changes in the industry have not been easy for local shopkeepers either. Cruise lines are cutting time in port to sell more on board, says one retailer. "They're becoming more rapacious–they want it all," he says. "They've developed vertical integration, from cruise fare to jewelry stores."

Local jewelry stores have been particularly hard hit. Jewelry stores that operate in ports of call around the world not only compete but bid up cost of downtown rent beyond the reach of many locally-owned businesses. Another long-established local downtown business owner was onboard a cruise where ship staff recommended stores affiliated with the cruise line as the only ones they could vouch for. "They (staff) didn't say 'don't shop local' directly, but by implication said local stores weren't trustworthy."

Blue is adamant: "We need to support the local businesses because the big boys will take care of themselves."

In the early 1990s I was planning itineraries for independent travelers, meeting clients at the airport or ferry terminals, shuttling them wherever they needed to go and introducing them to Juneau as I once did cruise ship passengers. My clients didn't know about the places I would have taken them in those earlier years, now off-limits to all but volume operators.

New tours gradually became available as growing numbers of tourists made them financially feasible. But something was lost, too—the flavor and juice, the choices and personal attention that small-scale locals brought to the mix.

Suddenly it was 1997. Hong Kong returned to Chinese rule. The bright lights of Mother Teresa and Princess Diana and John Denver passed into another dimension. The Hale-Bopp comet came closer to earth than it will be again until 4377. For my tour business it became a year of transition.

I knew I was in trouble when I met a couple at the Juneau Airport. He said nothing. She did not say hello.

"I want to speak to the manager of the airline," were her first words upon seeing me. They had requested special meals, and "the meat was too dry."

I had arranged the couple's itinerary at the request of a West Coast travel agent, who I later learned was their personal friend. My instinct had been to refuse to do this itinerary; normally I worked directly with travelers. I should have heeded my inner caution. The couple accused Anchorage hotels of not paying their bed tax; they wanted group discounts from small operators on a custom itinerary. When the woman was unhappy with her airline meal, their agent said that writing letters of complaint to get refunds is "what he does."

I shot back "I'm proud to say that working very hard to insure that people have a good experience in Alaska, based on their interests and special needs, is 'what I do.'"

It was nearly the first adversarial relationship I could recall in 13 years of business. But I could feel a change in the climate and it wasn't global warming.

In February of that year I was contacted about a 20th anniversary trip. Honeymoons, anniversaries, birthdays, end-of-life trips were all reasons people found themselves inside our vans. The Alaska-bound traveler asked how the experience would differ between a cruise with a major line and an itinerary I would design.

"I think you summed it up best in saying ours is a very personal approach," I wrote back. "In each location, our guests are met by their lodging host or tour operator. I personally meet our clients in Juneau. Our land travel is typically by mini-van or van rather than bus. Whenever appropriate, our cruise vessel is a charter boat.

"Our tours feel more like independent travel because you are not moving with the same group of people throughout. We also offer the chance to meet local residents throughout the trip, where you tend to meet primarily other travelers in large group travel."

He sent an email back: "We have complete flexibility. Go ahead and start finding out what is available."

The couple agreed to the itinerary I proposed. and sent a credit card number to use for deposit at wilderness lodges. A month later the man emailed a cut-and-paste spreadsheet calculating every single cost in dollars and cents, down to meals. To help them trim expenses I rewrote their itinerary, shortening full-day trips to half-day ones, and substituting ferry for air and van for rail.

When I met the couple at the airport, I felt a chill as though I was an adversary. After they returned home I sent my usual letter: "Welcome home. I hope you enjoyed your travels in Alaska," followed by my usual ending—"Thank you for letting me be a part of your travels in Alaska."

But the air had changed, as imperceptible but unmistakable as the day you know autumn has nudged summer aside.

Travel to Alaska became easy and common, and people looking for adventure were looking elsewhere.

Around 2000, stories began appearing in national press: "Alaska is getting crowded," wrote the *New York Times*. "Vacation from Hell," blared a travel column. ("It was tongue-in-cheek humor," the author said when contacted by our local tourism promoter, but Juneau wasn't laughing.)

Other factors came into play, of course. The web was coming to the average desktop. The internet changed everything for the travel industry. I'm not sure that even with the whole web before them, people found it any easier to understand the logistics of traveling Alaska on their own. Perhaps they were frustrated they hadn't been able to plan their trip by themselves, seeing just enough online to persuade them I was ripping them off.

Suddenly my clients saw me not as a friend but as an antagonist. I was working as hard as ever to insure a seamless trip, but half of them met me with an accusing demeanor.

"Who needs this?" I thought.

Blue had moved to Petersburg (8 hours away by Alaska Marine Highway) in 1995, and was no longer operating her tour business. I missed her wit, her energy and enthusiasm, and the camaraderie we shared.

Running a business takes both vision and a keen sense of finance. For the sole proprietor it can be hard to embody the fire and aptitude for both. I'd look at the carefully sorted file folders labeled with customers' last names, their itineraries stapled inside the front cover. I was working 12-hour days, on the short six-foot commute from bedroom to home office. How much more could I physically do? If I can just handle more customers, I thought, I could make real money, though I was reluctant to make the next big step to hiring employees and the increased volume I'd need to sustain them. In the end it wouldn't have mattered. Defunct travel agencies around the country bear witness to that.

I would continue planning tours for a few more years, but it was clearly time to think about moving on. Wal-Mart had moved into the neighborhood.

23. Reclaiming the Exclamation Point

Even ardent tourism boosters admit it. Some of the wow is gone. People still seem to enjoy their trips to Alaska, but it's not quite the once-in-a-lifetime destination it once was.

For many people it has gone from wild to mild. Frontier towns have become burnished renditions of their earlier selves. It no longer seems as appropriate to say "Alaska!" At least it's not a given. When the state marketing association came up with a 2005 billboard campaign in the form of Alaska's blue and gold license plate proclaiming "Alaska B4UDIE," advertising analysts called it bold and edgy. The first director of the now-defunct Alaska Tourism Marketing Council, currently living outside the state, called it "without doubt the tackiest promotion I've ever seen the state endorse." It seemed to some of us like a last gasp to hold on to an era that has ceased to exist.

On a six-ship day in Juneau, with some 14,500 people in port including passengers and crew, a woman from New York likened the disgorged masses to Grand Central Station. Lured north by eyeball-close photos of wildlife in wilderness settings, it's not perhaps what most expected to find.

The travel industry is partly to blame, relying on glossy clichés and unrealistic expectations as though the truth of Alaska were not enough. Travel writers are often complicit, buying into it with articles that are too perky and glib. We should hold them to the same level of accuracy we expect of other journalists. An article in an automotive club magazine, admittedly in the business of selling cruises, spewed so many untruths I pulled out a yellow marker to keep track of them:

> Cruise ships are the transportation of choice when it comes to spotting brown bears, polar bears, salmon, otters and bald eagles as they swim, romp and swoop along the thousands of miles of coastline waters you'll pass on your journey.

Until sea ice recedes even more off the north coast of Alaska, cruise ships won't come within a thousand miles of a polar bear. And by then the bear may be driven to extinction by lack of food and habitat. If you read the the short article accompanying the main story, you'll learn you'd have to fly to an Inupiat village on the Beaufort Sea 250 miles north of the Arctic Circle. It doesn't mention that during cruise ship season most polar bears are still far off shore on the ice pack. That could be a good thing. Of all of Alaska's bears, polar bears are the least to be trifled with. The interagency Alaska Public Lands Information Center issues this caveat:

> WARNING: Polar bears are extremely dangerous. There have been several deaths and maulings by polar bears coming directly into villages and field camps. A standard passenger vehicle is not a guarantee of safety against polar bears. They are unafraid of humans and may attack them as prey. At this time there are no special facilities or vehicles for safely viewing polar bears in these communities.

You could see brown bear if you were in port long enough to fly into a stream where they're feeding on spawning salmon—and if you booked the charter flight on your own long before your cruise departure. And you came during salmon runs between mid-July and mid-August. Salmon and eagles are pretty visible in port calls if you get away from the ship, but pretty distant from aboard a cruise ship at sea.

> The perpetually curious gray whale is most likely to stop by. Known for their propensity to "check out" ships, it provides a great photo op for onboard guests as they surface from the cool sapphire waters.

Gray whales spend their summers in the Bering and Chukchi Seas off the west coast of Alaska, heading south to Baja in October and returning north early to mid-April. After mid-May, when most Alaska cruises begin, they'll be far north of cruise ship routes. Independent travelers could, however, book gray whale cruises from late March through mid-May when they're migrating along the south Alaska coast.

> The winding, 20-mile train ride on the White Pass & Yukon Route Railroad is precisely the same route taken by those seeking their fortune in the 1890s, but your time in Skagway might be best served with a more adventuresome trek, such as dog sledding.

"Winding" only faintly describes the rail excursion which we book for all our own visiting family and friends.

> The heart-stopping exhilaration of dog mushing past herds of caribou, otters and the like is hard to beat.

Well, it would be heart-stopping. Caribou summer on the coastal plain of the high Arctic, hundreds of miles from Skagway. Otters are no more likely to be anywhere near dog mushing tours.

> Pre-and post-stays provide an opportunity to at least attempt a trek up the 20,320-foot-high Mt. McKinley.

Even the least-informed would not buy into that.

When a travel columnist from Florida wrote an account of her disappointing search for Alaska's elusive wildlife, I wrote her directly, pouring out my philosophy of travel to this place.

"The *Juneau Empire* recently published your account of your disappointing search for Alaska's elusive wildlife," I wrote.

"Yet your article itself contained the kernels of information to create a very different experience.

"John Muir, John McPhee, Joe McGinnis all paint compelling word pictures of their travels in Alaska. All traveled out-of-the way places in the company of Alaskans. While most visitors do not have the luxury of spending as much time in Alaska as these articulate observers, great adventures, and even wildlife, await travelers who part from the crowds. Small lodges, sailing and motorized charter boats, charter aircraft, sightseeing vans are operated by year-around Alaskans who feel passionately about their home state and go more than the extra mile to share it with visitors.

"It is true that wildlife sightings can never be guaranteed. Wild creatures are never far away, though their presence is not always obvious. Weather, ocean tides, seasonal changes, nature's own rhythms and willingness to meet nature on her terms will all affect the species that people observe.

"Still, there are ways to improve your odds of seeing wild creatures. If you wish to observe a particular species, learn all you can about it in advance. Know its habitat, its habits, and where you're apt to find it during the season of your visit.

"When you look around in search of wildlife, take in large areas at once. Watch for movement, then focus in. Look for parts of an animal or bird, because it may be partly obscured. From a distance, animals will appear smaller than you expect them to look.

"All our communities along the Inside Passage are small, and wild areas are never more than a few blocks away.

"The travel industry has a propensity for filling every brochure with close-up photos of animals that are rarely if ever visible to large groups traveling together. Some are so elusive they are rarely seen at all. For some people it is enough merely to know that these creatures live unfettered in Alaska, even if they never see them.

For those who truly want a closer look, and will meet nature on her own terms, Alaska is filled with wonders and surprises."

I did not get a response.

The wow is still here, of course. As S. Hall Young wrote in his autobiography, *Hall Young of Alaska*, "Alaska views need both eyes and a soul to see them."

Young was a Presbyterian missionary to Wrangell, and developed a friendship with John Muir about as unlikely as my friendship with Blue. Young was a cleric, Muir had little use for organized religion and found his gospel and salvation in nature. But they shared a love of the outdoors and literature and a bond that began with their first handshake, a friendship so strong and warm that Young would write that the day Muir sailed into Wrangell was the greatest event of his life in Alaska.

Young described three sets of eyes on one of his cruises returning from Glacier Bay, no doubt with Muir also aboard. Young saw "a thousand milk-white waterfalls leaping from mountain breasts; fairy-like islands peering from enchanting vistas. . . all of it a thrilling phantasmagoria, enough to lift one's soul from his body!"

On deck a young man came to Young's side, asking about all the scenery they were supposed to see. It was nothing but a repetition of the same thing, he complained, just islands and ice and mountains and water. A century later, I met a man from Chicago disembarking a ferry at Auke Bay.

242

"How are you enjoying your trip?" I said with our customary cheeriness. "It's the most boring place I've ever seen," he responded. "There's nothing but mountains and snow and trees."

Next Young encountered a vivacious young woman, still in her teens, calling to a friend to come see a waterfall.

"Yes–pretty isn't it?" the friend replied, urging her to come back to finish their casino game.

Then Young climbed to the upper deck and saw a man he'd met two days earlier who had been introduced as an English nobleman. Young recalled the Englishman was standing statuesque and motionless, looking toward the mountains. Young started to speak to him, then noticed tears streaming from his eyes and trickling down his beard.

"Here was a silence I could not break," Young wrote. "Here was an inner sanctuary I must not enter." He paused; they stood apart, and communed in silence.

"Alaska views need both eyes and a soul to see them."

"Get away from the crowds," I'd tell my passengers. Go to a restaurant frequented by locals. Pick up a local newspaper–a straightforward way to immerse yourself in the local culture for mere coin. While everyone else is walking straight ahead, veer to the left or right, or turn in the opposite direction. Walk a quiet trail. Stand on a vacant stretch of beach. Still places, even today, are often a block or two away and there are local greeters everywhere to point the way. Just be open, listen and feel, I'd say. If they'd still ask why I lived here after a day or two of following my counsel, I thought, they wouldn't understand the answer.

While hosting a *Prairie Home Companion* cruise in 2006, Garrison Keillor wrote what many of us thought more than two decades earlier: "A cruise ship is the lazy man's way to see the wilderness." Yet he understood that what is obscene to a hiker on the mountain path–the sight of a luxury liner in the bay below—is perversely pleasant to the people aboard—so pleasant that numbers of cruise ship travelers to Juneau had grown from 125,000 in 1984 to nearly a million when Keillor penned his thoughts.

When the accessible wilderness becomes that accessible, it's easy to imagine Alaska as subdued as a Midwest cornfield. Adventure travel destinations scarcely mention it anymore, as though the wildness is gone.

It's not, of course. Wildness is literally outside the window. A long-time resident, avid boater and boating safety advocate was returning his 14-foot skiff to the dock late one Sunday afternoon when he slipped on a small pool of oil, hit his head and fell into 43-degree water. He judged that he swam for an hour to reach the nearest land, an uninhabited island, and spent the night wracked with chills and plagued by clouds of mosquitoes. When he was found by a rescue dog 17 hours later he was seriously hypothermic and might not have survived much longer. Yet the island is visible from his house.

When I was planning custom itineraries I encouraged people to make their own discoveries between the pre-reserved activities. In the end our surprise encounters create some of our strongest memories for it is the unexpected that delights us and adds sparkle to our lives.

Sometimes it seems that travel television and the internet and designer brochures rob us of those secret pleasures in travel. We see a kangaroo and think "Oh, that's just how I thought it would look." Or we've already seen an architectural marvel displayed from so many angles in so many books and calendars that there's little to discover on our own.

When my husband and I traveled in Australia, the most memorable parts of the trip were William Ricketts' sanctuary, which we'd never heard of before arriving, and the Victorian Arts Theatre complex, which we'd never seen in photographs and knew nothing of save its name.

Ricketts' sanctuary is designed around the essence of personal discovery. As visitors walk through a fern-filled forest, each turn of the path reveals yet another clay sculpture inspired by the indigenous desert Pitjantjara and Arrernte people with whom he lived. Faces and busts and full statues blend with the forest itself, expressing his belief that "all life is one."

The theater complex is not particularly dramatic above ground. If I had seen photos of its tactile, opulent interior and state of the art performance space I might not have been as tempted inside because on a printed page they would have surely fallen far short of their full dimensional reality.

We expected the Sydney Opera House to be a highlight of our trip. After seeing it in dozens of photos, my most memorable image will be the way it was illuminated at night. One night the mélange of colored lights swirling over its surface created a paisley design. A paisley opera house— something I'd never seen before or envisaged—became my most enduring image of this incredible landmark.

My fondest hope for my clients was that they, too, would make unexpected discoveries and count them as highlights of their travels in Alaska.

24. Our First Season Ends

When that first summer yielded to autumn in 1984, Blue and I left the streets with a sense of relief that we were veterans of our first season.

I didn't know much about the Aviator's life away from the dock. It was the last time I would see him. He drove cab around Juneau for a while through fall and winter. Later we heard he had moved out of town.

How many years has it been now? His image is as vivid as on the summer days we jostled for the best parking spot and customers. Am I still confronting this dark side of myself? I vowed never to let someone affect me that way again.

Each summer we would be joined by new tour operators. Some stayed for just a season, like the newlyweds we called The Honeymooners. They might have stepped off the top of a cake, he in a white shirt and formal jacket, she in long flowered print dress. They filled a small clear vase with fresh wildflowers and attached it to a back window of their black 1955 Jaguar, which garnered constant attention from travelers. After a summer on the streets they turned their attention to careers in the newly developing internet and to starting a family. The Jag was sold when their growing family needed the garage space it occupied.

It seemed at times romance was all around. Another newly-married woman stayed on the sidewalk to sell the tours her husband provided first by taxi and later by bus. When people stopped to talk she told them about her new marriage and her man. "He's Mr. Wonderful," she'd gush as they smiled and we rolled our eyes. Thus we called him Mr. Wonderful as yet another shorthand nickname was born.

The Kid, with a van like mine, quickly decided this was no way to make a living. The rest of us would continue to meet visitors for varying numbers of seasons.

In the fall of 2002, five months after Blue and I met the first ship and shared our memories in May, I returned to the dock for the season's last sailing in September. It was a late sailing, added to recoup lost revenue after an onboard virus in peak season had forced cancellations while the infected ship was docked and scrubbed down. Hundreds of passengers and dozens of crew had left feeling as if they had their worst day of the flu. The virus couldn't have come at a worse time; the travel industry was still in the post 9/11 slump and every dollar mattered.

At least 10 shops had already taped newsprint and brown paper over storefront windows. Some stores had closed to move to a new location in the spring. Others offered 10, 40, 60 percent off. One of the former fine art galleries had given in to trinkets, photo mats with openings spelling ALASKA in block letters, a Hawaiian style shirt with the faces of husky sled dogs, glass jars of red and yellow chili peppers in vinegar.

Remembering the galleries that once thrived here, it was a sad evolution. At summer's end, life was draining from this four-block stretch. If this were the emergency room, flatline would be imminent. The local shopkeepers were tired from tourists. The locals were tired of tourists. The collective energy of a few hundred late season cruisers could not even raise a blip on the screen, let alone resuscitate this section of downtown.

It was cold on this morning—not the damp chill of a rainy fall day, but the chill that foretells winter, air with snow in it. It was one of those days when you knew there was fresh snow on the mountaintops without even looking up. At my house, two miles from the glacier, the big round outdoor thermometer read 32 degrees.

I wore wool pants, a long-sleeved mock turtle, long-sleeve blouse, waterproof windproof jacket, knit muffler, and knit gloves. And I was cold. Wishing for earmuffs and a warmer jacket, I smiled. The cruisers would go home feeling they had seen the real Alaska.

October arrived a day later as . . . well, October. The frost had left the air; now there was just rain, hard rain. Winds were forecast. Yellow street lights reflected bright yellow orbs and streamers of light on the rain-shined streets.

It was municipal election day and the locals were reclaiming their town. Candidates and their supporters clustered at intersections along the commuter routes into the downtown core, waving and holding campaign signs as water streamed off hooded rain jackets. We all knew we had come home, and we felt alive.

Our attention would turn to our local symphony orchestra, lyric opera, repertory theater, school activities, dance groups, movies, books, and club meetings of every stripe. We'd support the arts as audience or participants, we'd read or write books, we'd turn our passions to politics.

Somewhere further up the Inside Passage, the cruise ship passengers who had walked Juneau's streets in cool comfort the day before were awakening to the truth of the rainforest. Tall, thick stands of evergreens, endless waterfalls and countless streams come at a price. "That's why we call it a rainforest," I would have said when I was leading tours. They would tell each other that yes, Alaska was beautiful, but wouldn't it be great to get back home. And why would anyone want to live there?

Many of us would continue watching the natural world that summer travelers would miss.

From my diary, October 10, 2000:

A twisting, undulating, iridescent pearl ribbon against a drear gray sky. Moving southeast, then north, then circling back. Following the shore of Douglas Island below the crest, then crossing over Gastineau channel to soar high over Blackerby Ridge, 3,500 feet or more. Gulls, we wondered at first sighting? Too large, too orderly, in V's that shifted and moved in and out of formation. Individuals weaving in front of each other as the V changed to a fractured cluster, then re-formed. I could imagine them with long satin streamers in their beaks, weaving a many-hued tapestry in the sky. At last we could see their graceful long necks and heard, only once, a distinctive honk of a swan. Were there 200 swans in transit from northern breeding grounds to the grain fields of the Pacific Northwest? Surely, well over 100. Would some linger for the winter at Petersburg's Blind Slough, to await our Audubon field trip in three weeks?

A gray October day, increasingly stormy, was transformed.

25. We Say Good-bye—September 2003

It was beyond rain, really; an angry, pelting thing. Few could fail to take umbrage at such a vicious attack. Drops fell with such vigor it seemed the rain gods were squeezing every opportunity out of their last chance. It wasn't their last chance, of course. This is the rain forest, after all. But the rain made its point. The walk we'd planned would wait.

Blue opted for a book, sprawled on the bed that would be hers for only two more nights, while I predictably retreated to my computer. I was designing her card and fussed endlessly over the layout. Where, exactly, should one photo overlap the other? Which font should I use for just eight words on the front? How should I highlight two main words—different colors? Bold face? In the end I decided on italics and underline, with vertical lines for emphasis. One red line, one blue line, 40 percent tint for softening.

The inside was easier—a quote about friendship from a favorite author, Kahlil Gibran. Then just the handwritten message remained. I typed out the words first, changing one then another. It had to be just right.

The next day was an unexpected gift—the kind someone brings you "just because." Customary late September rains yielded without notice to fog, then to the purest, bluest skies you could imagine.

Blue called. We could walk today. Her last-minute refrigerator clean-up would wait. She wrapped a sore knee for added strength.

The trail head at the airport wetlands had more cars than I'd ever seen. It was Sunday and working people were seizing the chance to be outside. Tourists were gone. The sun was warmer than on most summer days. It was a surreal, out-of-body kind of day.

Our notoriously evergreen world was surprisingly golden and red. Leafy stalks of fireweed that bloomed fuchsia in July were the color of pomegranates. Willow leaves were brassy yellow. Duck hunting season was open and the high tide floated canoes of camouflage-clad hunters.

Blue was moving back to Denver. Life was not easy for her here, a woman alone after the death of her husband. Her two adult daughters coaxed her south where they'd be close by, and bought a condo for her to live in. We walked and spoke of how she could afford to return for a visit if she escorted a tour group. We'd build her tour costs into their package price. They'd travel by ferry from Bellingham, stopping first at Petersburg, the fishing village where she had lived when she was widowed two and one-half years ago. Then to Juneau where they could choose between fishing, flight-seeing and shopping and she could steal away to visit friends spanning the decades of her life here.

I remembered some buttons I'd had made several years earlier when I was aggressively promoting my business. "Ask me about Alaska," they said in bold letters on pastel blue, green, yellow and pink backgrounds. I promised to look for them when I got home.

We stopped and found a log to sit on when the trail abruptly ended, covered by water of the high tide. When we gradually headed back to the trail head, she asked if we had time to go to the glacier.

"Sure," I said, without pointing out the obvious. It would be her last look at the destination that defined our years together on the street.

The warm sun on the wetlands trail was replaced by a light but cool breeze flowing from the glacier.

"The air is so different here," she said. We had driven a distance of only four miles. "It even smells different." She was right, of course. Maybe she'd always noticed that difference but I knew her senses would be heightened today. I wondered how I would feel on the day I knew I was making my last visit here. Then I shut the thought from my mind.

We walked to photo point, where we had gone countless times with visitors. "This could be your Christmas card photo," I said as she stood in front of the glacier.

She smiled and beckoned with a nod. She wanted her own picture taken here on this last day. I took my digital camera from a small black leather fanny pack and obliged.

"Do you want the glacier or the waterfall in the background?" I asked.

"I want it all."

As we walked the path back toward the parking lot, I noted my favorite place on the rocky outcrop, a sculpted pool perpetually filled with rainwater and snowmelt. Blue said that her grandson, now 31, had sat at the edge as a young teen visiting Alaska and still remembered this spot.

We looked for spawning salmon in Steep Creek. It was between runs and there were none. Then it was over, that golden afternoon.

I dropped her at her trailer for a final night, with a promise we would see each other at dinner tomorrow.

She wanted to say goodbye in her own way. Her last night in Juneau would be spent at a motel near the airport for her 6:20

a.m. departure. She'd call a taxi for a ride. No wrenching, teary good-byes at the airport for her.

The evening before her outbound flight, she hosted a small group of friends at dinner in a Mexican restaurant at the motel: two couples from the church she'd helped start, a picturesque little chapel in the woods; a couple living in an adjacent trailer who'd shared many of her ups and downs through 25 years of living; and me. It was easier than saying good-bye individually, she'd tell us.

"We have to all leave at the same time," I said to my fellow guests but really to myself.

There were gifts: a green amber necklace, a black Russian lacquer box inlaid with mother of pearl Northern Lights glowing above a colorful village scene.

A card from her longest-time friend that affectionately called her "sister." We all laughed—the card felt appropriate in every way even though the inside said "happy birthday."

I held my own card back. I'd give it to her just before we parted, along with a CD of classical music and sounds of nature I'd found in Skagway, and a journal for writers.

I wanted to linger after the others left, to share a final drink in the bar and hold on as long as possible. But I remembered some of my own painful good-byes—how I needed to fix my eyes ahead and not turn around.

We hugged at the edge of the parking lot.

"Here. Open this when you're on the plane or in Denver or someplace," I said. "Have a good trip. I'll see you in Denver in five or six months." I walked toward my car, and I didn't look back.

Back home I opened a Dove dark chocolate, the kind you can eat without conscience every day because it's good for you. I read the saying inside the red foil wrapper: "You know what? You look good in red."

253

26. Getting to Wistful

Seven years later it was my turn to make a last trip to the glacier that I could claim as two miles from my home. It was a sunny morning, May 30, 2010.

All of us have days that define our lives. I have book ends—Friday, August 13, 1965, the day I arrived in Alaska; Sunday, May 30, 2010, the day I left.

The process of leaving a home of 45 years gnawed around my consciousness for several years and began in earnest the year before I left.

It was not an easy nor smooth path.

We often identify with the place we call home. The way we attach to geography, whether natural or political, becomes part of the way we see ourselves, the essence of who we are. Alaska seems to stir that sense of identity in a way few other places do. When our place changes or is lost, it can cause a kind of grief, a loss as potent as any other. It is a grief not acknowledged as fully as it deserves. Loss of a house, yes. Loss of homeland, surely and rightfully so. But not loss of our sense of place.

The last Christmas when I could still claim two homes, the holiday card I traditionally design included photos from each and two quotes.

From Wendell Berry, "If I belonged *in* this place, it was because I belonged *to* it."

And from Russell Sanders, "I can not have a spiritual center without having a geographical one; I cannot live a grounded life without being grounded in a place. In belonging to a landscape, one feels a rightness, at-homeness, a knitting of self and world."

Someone asked me on a sunny day if it wouldn't be hard to leave Juneau on a day like that. It wouldn't. What will be hard is leaving on a misty, rainy, quintessential Southeast day—the kind that has always made me feel I was home.

I counted the things I will most miss:

Courtship call of the varied thrush.

Ravens.

Living five minutes from the airport.

Bullwinkle's Pizza.

Jerry's hams (Fred's nomination).

By mid-March, Juneau starts to slip between my fingers, like an open hand combing through sand. I'm gradually detaching. The day I departed thankfully brought bright sun and cloudless skies.

Settling into New York, I set out to re-invest in this new place as a full-time home. How can I do that without betraying the last 45 years, the great bulk of my adult life? It was that life that heightened my awareness of the natural world, from the minutia to the grand, where my identity was deeply intertwined with place. It made me who I am and it cannot be denied. I reach out to touch the fingertips of friendships that span decades, knowing that the longer we move in separate orbs, the less we will have in common. That fills me with longing.

Now I live in the aftermath of ancient glaciers. My house sits on what was Lake Warren, a precursor to Lake Erie that existed about 12,000-13,000 years ago. Deeper than the current Lake Erie, its shoreline extended about eight miles further inland. That once-lake-bed, a narrow strip of land two to six miles wide and 55 miles long, now sustains 30,000 acres of vineyards and two dozen wineries.

Little Canadaway Creek runs below the bank behind our house, sometimes nearly dry, sometimes too deep and swift to cross when swollen by rain at higher elevations. The water that courses nearby is headed toward Lake Erie, eventually to drop over Niagara Falls, flow into Lake Ontario, then the St.

24. Places I Have Lived
    Koeln, Germany
    Springen, now Heidenrod in the Taunus Mountains, Germany
    Wiesbaden in the Taunus Mountains
    Kyushu Island, Japan
    Kansas
    Arizona
    Colorado
    Alaska. I've never been in a place I've so fallen in love with.
    Of all the places that I have lived, every one of them has its own beauty and charm. I can close my eyes, smell the air and know where I am. Of course the sounds help, too. For instance, Koeln has a certain smell that is mixed with traffic and the water of the Rhine River.
    In Springen, clean country air will greet you, mixed with spruce and pine trees. To this day this place is like a resort, a Luftkurot, healthy air for people with asthma–lung complications.
    Wiesbaden, also a Luftkurot (spa), has about the same influence as Springen, only it lies higher and the air is cleaner yet, but there I miss the water. In Europe there is a different smell in the air than in the Far East and in the U.S.

Lawrence River and into the Atlantic Ocean. I try to remember and fathom we are custodians of a tiny piece of the earth's largest fresh surface water system.

From my porch, a breeze sweeping over Lake Erie three miles to the north sets greenery in motion. From here I survey my favorite summer things: white-edged hostas as wide as a yardstick, hydrangea shrubs covered with blooms mid-June into fall. Forget-me-nots bloom wild in our fields, as they do

---

Kansas, dry, dusty hot air, no water–a barren place and yet it has its own beauty. In Japan, hardly any traffic, mostly bikes in 1959. Had water, rivers and lakes, clean air. Arizona has clean dry desert air, humidity is very low. A certain smell of plants and flowers, no water except on its western border with the Colorado River and Lake Havasu.

Colorado has glaciers, great vistas, icy roads, big animals, hunting and fishing just like Alaska. Oil is also in abundance, but needs to be brought to surface.

It has a desert climate, hardly any humidity, unlike Alaska. Alaska, oh yes, that's the place where water and wind embrace, but it can also spell silence and solitude. It's the place where I spent most of my life. While revisiting, I close my eyes, smell the low tide with its decaying smell, then breathe the fresh sea air, and I feel fulfilled.

Seeing the glacier, which now has receded quite a bit, feeling the cooler air there is an experience that makes one feel alive. The clouds are forever changing, throwing shadows, which is great for photography. Oh, here is a patch o' blue, a painter's paradise. In spring you add the beautiful colorful flowers, those are scenes that one can only dream of. Alaska will always have a special place in my heart.

throughout Alaska. Although not a daily presence as they are in Juneau, sightings of bald eagles and black bear are not unheard of here. Finches, rose-breasted grosbeak, chickadees, nuthatch eat black oil sunflower seeds from a feeder handmade by our neighbor, Lloyd. It swings from a wrought iron tree that reminds me of winter-bare branches. Another of Lloyd's feeders holds a glass jar for grape jelly and and spikes for fresh orange slices, favorites of the outrageously vivid Baltimore Orioles.

A sense of place grows over time, like friendships. I still claim two worlds. After morning coffee with the local newspaper I retrieve from a box across Route 20, I turn to the internet and revisit two websites: *Anchorage Daily News* and *Juneau Empire.*

One morning the *Empire* published a reader-submitted letter about neighbor-to-neighbor phone call alerts that create a poetry of wildness, a poetry of place:

    Orcas in the Channel
    Bubblenetting at North Pass
    Goats galore on Juneau
    Butts biting at Handtroller's
    Bears out the Glacier
    Sockeyes strong at Sweetheart

I feel wistful. Just wistful. It is a milestone. Getting to wistful.

ABOUT THE AUTHORS

Judy Shuler now lives in rural Western New York and Hildegard Ratliff lives in Denver. Both carry Alaska in their hearts.

Made in the USA
Charleston, SC
26 May 2012